CONFIDENCE

A KEY TO VICTORIOUS LIVING

KEN SUMRALL

MorningStar
PUBLICATIONS
16000 Lancaster Highway • Charlotte, NC 28277-2061

This book is dedicated to

Wanda Sumrall

Who has been my wife, friend,
and companion for forty-seven years;

And to Johnny, Beth, Stanley and Marlene,
who are our children and special friends.

Contents

Foreword

"Therefore, do not throw away your confidence, which has a great reward" (Hebrews 10:35 NASB). Until I began reading the manuscript to this book, I did not realize just how much *confidence* the church had thrown away. Even more than that, I also began to understand why we have thrown it away, and how we can get it back. In this book, Ken Sumrall has captured the essence of something that we desperately need to recover.

There is a confidence that the world knows that is often depicted by a kind of strutting arrogance. There is a greater confidence that is rooted in the knowledge of God, which is revealed by the grace of true faith combined with the sublime dignity of godly humility. The former can keep the world somewhat agitated, the latter can lead the world out of darkness into the light. But rarely do we see the latter form, which may be one reason why the world remains in such darkness.

Every true spiritual advance in Scripture and history is the result of someone having had enough confidence in God to follow Him, usually against the masses who were going in another direction. Confidence involves faith, but it is actually a little deeper than that. We can have faith arise in our hearts to take certain immediate actions, but confidence is more of a long term constitution that sets the course of our life.

One of the most debilitating, long term failures of the modern evangelical movement has been its inability to combine the hope of the soon return of the Lord, with the effective strategic planning for the future. The result of this has been the drive to make quick converts rather than disciples with depth and character. This lack of depth breeds spiritual insecurity, which results in instability. In this modern, fast changing world, insecurity is now reaching epidemic proportions. We, the church, have been trusted with the answer to this most universal of modern maladies, but we ourselves must rediscover it first.

of one thing—battle! However, as Christians we are empowered to live as "more than conquerors." A true conqueror does not simply defend himself, he actually looks for battles in order to increase his territory. Every trial, or battle, that we encounter in life provides an opportunity to fight the good fight of faith; but only those with confidence will perceive them as such.

Confidence is also a key in discerning the will and victory God has for us. Confidence is a powerful word, and biblical confidence is a powerful grace. Some of the most powerful scriptural teachings surround this word, yet it is rarely discussed by modern day Bible teachers.

The apostle Paul said, **"Overwhelming victory is ours through Christ, who loved us enough to die for us" (Romans 8:37 TLB).** This verse reflects the depth and power of a conviction that was the foundation of the apostle's life. Despite distress, persecution, tribulation, famine, nakedness, peril and sword, Paul lived above it all as more than a conqueror. We, too, can live as more than conquerors because Jesus conquered and spoiled Satan at Calvary (see Colossians 2:15). Living according to the power of this great truth yields the power to live an overcoming life. The victory of the cross is the source of our confidence.

Suppose a boxer wins a championship fight, and, while healing from his wounds, he gives his wife the check for his winnings. He is a conqueror; she is *more* than a conqueror. He fought the opponent and won the victory; she reaped the benefits. Just so, Jesus conquered the devil at the cross and put him to open shame. Our Lord not only overcame the enemy, He bore the consequence of sin, took our wounds, and died in our place. He then rose again and now lives forever in victory. He did the fighting and then gave us the check! Our confidence is found in knowing that we are the bride of the Champion, and that His check is good. We can now boldly claim the benefits of His triumph—overwhelming victorious lives here and now in addition to eternal life with Him forever. The confidence we have in our relationship with the Lord surely reaps "a great reward."

Our goal as believers should be to lay such a solid, biblical foundation that our lives are full of confidence, and therefore, *victory.* The central bedrock of this truth is the relationship we have with Christ. It is true that we have the check for all His winnings, but even more than that, we have the Champion Himself within us. We have Jesus, the Christ, the Son of God, the Lord of lords and King of kings—and no one will ever take His title! The Church is His wife; He loves us more than any husband ever loved his bride. And He has shared His complete victory and His reward with us.

Biblical confidence is what enables a successful pastor to lead his flock with strategy and vision to reach a fallen world, to push back the powers of darkness and rescue those who are perishing from the grip of the enemy. It takes confidence to counsel, preach, pray for the sick, and comfort those who mourn. But confidence is not only vital for church leaders; it is vital for every Christian. *God wants you to live your life with confidence!*

Parents who trust in God plant confidence and security in their children. One of the greatest inspirations in my life was my mother. She was confident even in the times of the most severe pressures. She gave birth to and cared for eight children during the Great Depression, and when the cupboard was almost bare, and money was scarce, we saw peace on her face. Her constant encouraging words to us were: "Everything's all right. God will see us through." Because she was so confident, we felt so secure that we did not even know we were poor and "under-privileged" until we were grown!

Confidence to Jump over a Wall

King David declared: **"You have turned on my light! Now in your strength I can scale any wall and attack any troop" (Psalm 18:28,29 TLB).** This bold statement came after his troops charged and took Jerusalem from the boastful Jebusites who had dared him to try to scale their walls. *"Even the lame and blind can keep you from scaling our walls,"* they had scoffed (see II Samuel 5:6). David not only took the fortified city, but declared it to be his headquarters, and the fortress was thereafter called "The City of David." Likewise, some of the greatest obstacles of your life can become the place where your authority to rule in this life is established. God has not given us "a spirit of intimidation, but of power, love and a sound mind." When the enemy is scoffing, it is the time for attack, not timidity.

David's victory over the Jebusites was no surprise to him. His confidence had been established in his ability in the Lord when he was a shepherd lad. When facing Goliath, he exclaimed to Saul:

> **Don't worry about a thing... I'll take care of this Philistine...When I am taking care of my father's sheep... and a lion or a bear comes and grabs a lamb from the flock, I go after it with a club and**

take the lamb from its mouth. If it turns on me I catch it by the jaw and club it to death. I have done this to both lions and bears, and I'll do it to this heathen Philistine too, for he has defied the armies of the living God! The Lord who saved me from the claws and teeth of the lion and the bear will save me from this Philistine! (I Samuel 17:32-37 TLB).

To his older brother David sounded cocky, but the bold statements were not declared in arrogance—David was speaking out of strong inner conviction when he spoke those fearless words. There is a difference between biblical confidence and arrogance. Our confidence is not based in who we are, but in who *Christ is in us,* and what He has already accomplished through His victory at Calvary and His ever present high priestly ministry for us. This confidence is deeper and more powerful than any human confidence. Cockiness is shallow and shackled with a most repulsive character flaw—self-centeredness. Biblical confidence is full of grace and truth, and encompasses one of the most appealing characteristics that we can possess—the true humility of Christ-centeredness.

David was confident in fighting the Philistine champion, Goliath, because he knew that His God was greater than the gods of the Philistines. God rewarded his confidence with victory over the giant. David wrote of his great appreciation and adoration of the Lord:

What a God He is! How perfect in every way! All His promises prove true... He fills me with strength and protects me wherever I go. He gives me the surefootedness of a mountain goat upon the crags. He leads me safely along the top of the cliffs (Psalm 18:30,32,33 TLB).

Satan Flees from Bold Believers

If the Devil can neutralize your confidence, he knows he can nullify your witness and consign you to depression and defeat. On the other hand, he recognizes he has no power or authority over a confident believer. When you face the enemy with boldness, he will flee. As Peter exhorted, **"Submit therefore to God. Resist the devil and he will flee from you"(James 4:7 NASB).**

Since we believe it is true that the Church has authority over the devil, why is it then that our rebukes against the enemy have seemed so powerless in recent times? Perhaps we have not been obedient to God. Our authority comes from the Lord, which is why James said to first "submit to God," and then "resist the devil." As we draw close to the Lord, we will have increasing authority and confidence over the enemy. Our spiritual authority is based on faith in the Lord, and we are powerless when we lose the confidence that comes from being close to Him.

The prolonged retreat of the church before the march of secular humanism into every sphere of our society is the result of a loss of confidence by the church. We have been put on the defensive, but we should be on the offensive. God has called us to be conquerors and conquerors are always on the offensive.

We were promised that the gates of hell shall not prevail against the church (see Matthew 16:18). This was just after Peter declared his revelation that Jesus was the Christ, the Son of the Living God. It is this foundational revelation of who Jesus is that the enemy cannot prevail against. The deeper this revelation has prevailed in us, the greater our authority will be to prevail over the enemy.

We must recover our genuine expectation in the Lord's promise to confirm the gospel message with signs following. The Lord confirms His Word when it is spoken boldly under the anointing of the Holy Spirit. Without this holy boldness, based on confidence in who Christ is, and in our relationship to Him, the devil and the world will laugh and ignore us. The power of the gospel is not in just pronouncing the words, but in pronouncing them out of the deep conviction that comes from a revelation of who Jesus is.

The sons of Sceva were defeated by the devil though they may have been using the right words to try to cast out the demons. Neither our tone of voice nor our volume will affect demons. The depth of our revelation of Christ is the critical issue. The sons of Sceva declared to an evil spirit, **"I adjure you by Jesus whom Paul preaches."** The evil spirit answered: **"I recognize Jesus, and I know about Paul, but who are you?" (Acts 19:13,15 NASB).** The demonized man overpowered them and they fled in humiliation. Obviously, it takes more than the correct words to cast out demons. The sons of Sceva did not have authority against the enemy because they did not have a direct relationship to Jesus—they were trying to preach in the name of Jesus whom Paul knew, not whom they knew. That will never work. But if we do know Him, and are joined to Him, then Luke 10:19 will be true for us: **"Behold, I have given you authority to tread upon serpents and scorpions, and over all the power of the enemy, and nothing shall injure you" (NASB).**

The Lord continued this statement with a very important conclusion: **"Nevertheless do not rejoice in this, that the spirits are subject to you, but rejoice that your names are recorded in heaven" (Luke 10:20 NASB).** This is a warning to not become overly focused on chasing demons, but to always keep foremost the rejoicing in our relationship to Him, overjoyed that our names are recorded in His book.

Judgment Begins at the House of God

A few years ago the charismatic renewal was at its peak and television superstar preachers were watched and supported by millions around the world. It was prestigious to be a "Spirit-filled Christian." The cross and the "full" gospel had lost their stigma to the world. Conservative Christians of the evangelical and charismatic persuasions helped elect Ronald Reagan as President of the United States. It seemed that happy days were here to stay. Many declared the eighties would be times of even greater outpourings of the Holy Spirit on the churches of our nation. Though the Lord continued to bless churches who followed His Word and His will, the predicted refreshing for the whole body of Christ did not occur. Instead we experienced one of the most shameful times of humiliation and seeming defeat in the history of Christianity.

What was not discerned by some in church leadership was that much of the ministry of the time was not based on truth and genuine confidence in God's Word, but in impure ambitions and carnal motives. We had forgotten God's hatred of greed, selfish ambition, pride, disunity, dishonesty, and guile. Even sexual immorality was found to be widespread among some famous ministers.

Besides these offenses, some charismatic and evangelical streams had become somewhat exclusive and militantly defensive of their theological dogma. The so called "holy wars"among some top television personalities grew tragically by the eighties. One even used his popular television show to attack those who disagreed with his own convictions. Then, to the dismay of the nation, some who were ministering to extremely large television audiences were exposed and confessed to sexual indiscretion. When Saul fell into witchcraft and was killed, David cried: **"How are the mighty fallen! Tell it not in Gath, publish it not..." (II Samuel 1:19b,20 NASB).** Some of us cried the same about our brethren who had fallen. *"How the mighty have fallen... tell it not to the enemies and to the unchurched world."* But alas, it was told by the media and everywhere else. They took great delight in headlining the scandals around the world.

Stormy winds of doubt and confusion were blowing over this nation as the nineties began. The confidence of multitudes was shaken, and a spirit of gloom and defeat hovered over them. Some drifted into disillusionment, apathy and unbelief. But in the midst of our confusion, the Lord was not nervously wringing his hands! He knew all along that this great humiliation was necessary and, as always, He knew He would ultimately be glorified and that His church would benefit from it all.

However, we must learn the important lessons of these times, and one of the most serious is that the line between biblical confidence and spiritual arrogance can be very thin. It is not hard to discern the differences, but it can be an easy line to cross. We must repeat what has already been stated: The crucial difference is found in whether our confidence is self-centered or God-centered. If our confidence is truly God-centered, He will stand with us and He will also receive glory for our victories.

Beyond Success

True, biblical confidence will work whether a believer lives in a poor third-world country, or in an affluent wealthy society. God's word simply works anywhere its seeds are planted in the hearts of believers. A person's wealth, or lack thereof, does not reflect his depth of commitment to the Lord, and therefore cannot determine the measure of his confidence and his victories.

It is true that many of the principles used in our nation to promote success originated in kingdom laws revealed in the Scriptures. Biblical principles work in the sense that financial seeds reap financial fruit. That is scriptural and worthy of pursuit if kept in proper perspective. All else being equal, Christians should be the most successful people in their communities. We are exhorted to do everything that we do "as unto the Lord"and if we obey that directive, our work will be outstanding and will produce superior fruit after its kind.

Many books have been published in recent years to help people build their self-esteem. Some of these writings are scriptural and balanced. We should feel good about ourselves, if our hope and expectations are based on God's purpose and will for our lives. On the other hand, if we are self-centered and ambitious to merely portray a good self image or to just acquire material well-being, God's kind of confidence will be drastically lacking. We must have a Bible-based perception of ourselves which, to every member of the household of God, having been born with His image, will be a positive perception.

Notwithstanding, we should go beyond the desire for a good self-image, or even a legitimate desire for success, and focus our devotion on doing the will of God. Only then can we enter the place of divine rest, finding peace in all the storms of life and, in the process, conquering every enemy that hinders the church. We will then be filled with divine energy, joy, and a godly certainty in our inner man. Being in the will of God gives us the confidence to leap over every obstacle and send the devil fleeing. It is in this place of confidence that we can testify with the apostle: **"I can do everything God asks me to with the help of Christ who gives me the strength and power" (Philippians 4:13 TLB).** It is this Christ-centered confidence that must be recovered by the church if we are to accomplish our last day ministry.

Chapter Two

Foundations for Confidence

Watching a few hours of television will quickly confirm that the real product most advertisers are trying to sell us is *confidence*. Whether the product is soap, breath mints, or athletic shoes, we are promised increased confidence just by its usage. While some of these products can help raise our level of confidence in certain situations, they will never be able to appease the depths of our real need for it. The Bible directs us to the place of our real need:

> **It is better to trust in the Lord than to put confidence in man. It is better to trust in the Lord than to put confidence in princes (Psalm 118:8-9).**

> **In the fear of the Lord is strong confidence: and his children shall have a place of refuge (Proverbs 14:26).**

Businesses may have rightly discerned that the search for confidence is common to man. Certainly no individual or business enterprise can function effectively without some degree of confidence. It is clear that the greater our confidence, the more effectively we can function. However, we must be careful that our confidence is properly placed, or we too will end up in the disappointment experienced by everyone who places their confidence in men.

Billions of dollars are spent each year by a world seeking what Christians have been freely given. Even so, many Christians spend their lives in doubt and fear because, having been carried away by the worldly pursuit of confidence, they too only experience a shallow substitute. Substitutes may look, feel or taste like the reality, but they are a counterfeit. The confidence that the Lord gives to us is not like the world's confidence; it is much greater. It cannot be attained by the same methods through which the confidence of this world is attained.

Definitions of Confidence

We must understand the real confidence of God if we are going to walk in it. According to the Reader's Digest book of synonyms, *Use the Right Word*, confidence refers to "a psychological trait that involves a conviction of one's own worth or an unselfconscious certainty of succeeding at whatever is attempted, unhampered by doubt, hesitation, or fear."[1] That is a good definition of what the world considers confidence, but we cannot use Reader's Digest as an authority for spiritual truth. This kind of confidence can easily develop into cockiness or self-assurance, or what we, personally, can do in our own strength, intelligence, or because of our religious heritage.

Confidence does come from believing that all is or will be well, but the source of this confidence is crucial. The word may also suggest fearless trust, whether well or ill-advised. Oral Roberts once defined confidence as "standing up on the inside." This is what we want to do, but we want to be standing up on the inside for the right reasons—because God is our salvation and strength, and He will never leave us or forsake us.

Another definition of confidence is "internal security." This can only come when all is well with you and the Lord, and also well with your relationships with others. This is also the result of knowing, and living within, your own gifts, purposes and limitations. We all need, and want, that kind of confidence. Paul strongly asserted: **"... we... put no confidence in the flesh" (Philippians 3:3 NASB)** and **"nothing good dwells in me, that is, in my flesh" (Romans 7:18 NASB)**. Our confidence must be in the Lord who desires to reveal Himself in us, and to make us aware of who we are in Him.

Old Testament Confidence

Psalm 112:7-8 gives us a picture of a person with godly confidence:

> **He shall not be afraid of evil tidings: his heart is fixed, trusting in the Lord.**
>
> **His heart is established, he shall not be afraid, until he see his desire upon his enemies.**

Overall the word "confidence" appears thirty-eight times in the Bible, eighteen in the Old Testament and twenty in the New Testament. There are eight other references to the word "confident" throughout Scripture. Countless other passages indirectly imply confidence.

In the Hebrew language, there are seven different words which can be translated as confidence. They are:

(1) **Betach**, which means "confidence" or "trust," and is found in Ezekiel 28:26:

> **And they shall dwell safely therein, and shall build houses, and plant vineyards; yea, they shall dwell with confidence, when I have executed judgments upon all those that despise them round about them; and they shall know that I am the Lord their God.**

(2) **Bitchah**, which also means "confidence" or "trust," and occurs in Isaiah 30:15:

> **For thus saith the Lord God, the Holy One of Israel; In returning and rest shall ye be saved; in quietness and in confidence shall be your strength: and ye would not.**

(3) **Bittachon,** which can be translated both "confidence" and "trust." It is found in II Kings 18:19 and is repeated again in Isaiah 36:4:

> **And Rabshakeh said unto them, Say ye now to Hezekiah, Thus saith the great king, the king of Assyria, What confidence is this *wherein thou trustest?***

(4) *Kesel*, which means "firmness" or "stoutness" and is also translated "confidence." It is found in Proverbs 3:26:

For the Lord shall be thy confidence, and shall keep thy foot from being taken.

(5) *Kislah*, which also means "firmness" or "stoutness" and is translated "confidence." It appears in Job 4:6:

Is not this thy fear, thy confidence, thy hope, and the uprightness of thy ways?

(6) *Mibtach*, which means "confidence" and "trust" and appears in nine different Old Testament verses: Job 18:14; Job 31:24; Psalm 65:5; Proverbs 14:26; Proverbs 21:22; Proverbs 25:19; Jeremiah 2:37; Jeremiah 48:13. A good example of how this is used is found in Ezekiel 29:16:

And it shall be no more the confidence of the house of Israel, which bringeth their iniquity to remembrance, when they shall look after them: but they shall know that I am the *Lord God*.

(7) *Batach* which means "to be confident" or "to have trust." It also occurs in Psalms 118:8-9; Micah 7:5; Judges 9:26; Proverbs 14:16. This is the word used in Psalm 27:3:

Though an host should encamp against me, my heart shall not fear: though war should rise against me, in this will I be confident (Psalm 27:3).

New Testament Confidence

In the New Testament, there are five Greek words which are translated confidence:

(1) *Parrhesia* means "boldness" or "free-spokenness" and is found in six verses: Acts 28:31; Hebrews 3:6; Hebrews 10:35; I John 2:28; I John 3:21. This is the word used in I John 5:14:

> **And this is the confidence that we have in him, that, if we ask any thing according to *his will, he heareth us.***

(2) *Pepoithesis* means "confident" or "persuasion" and is found in five different verses: II Corinthians 1:15; II Corinthians 10:2; II Corinthians 8:22; Ephesians 3:12. A good example of the usage of this word is in Philippians 3:4:

> **Though I might also have confidence in the flesh. If any other man thinketh that he hath whereof he might trust in the flesh, I *more.***

(3) *Hupustasis* means "a quality of confidence that leads one to stand, endure or undertake anything; a standing under; a substratum." It appears in II Corinthians 11:17. This is also the word used in Hebrews 3:14:

> **For we are made partakers of Christ, if we hold the beginning of our confidence stedfast unto the end.**

(4) *Tharrheo* means "to have good courage" and appears in II Corinthians 7:16:

I rejoice therefore that I have confidence in you in all things.

(5) *Peitho* means "to persuade" and is found in II Corinthians 2:3; Galatians 5:10; Philippians 1:25; II Thessalonians 3:4; Philemon 21; and in Philippians 3:3:

For we are the circumcision, which worship God in the spirit, and rejoice in Christ Jesus, and have no confidence in the flesh.

Another form of the verb *peitho* also means to "wax confident" or "to persuade." It appears only in Philippians 1:14:

And many of the brethren in the Lord, waxing confident by my bonds, are much more bold to speak the word without fear.

These together give a sound biblical definition for the word "confidence," and the importance that God places on it. This is the foundation from which we seek to grasp that which is true confidence, and to recognize and avoid that which may be a humanistic substitute.

Chapter Three

Seven Sources of Confidence

The prophet Isaiah makes a splendid declaration of the all-encompassing provision of God in Isaiah 30:15, but the verse concludes with a frightful decision made by the people of Judah:

For thus saith the Lord God, the Holy One of Israel; In returning and rest shall ye be saved; in quietness and in confidence shall be your strength: *and ye would not.*

Interestingly, God is offering a provision of strength and safety to His people. Yet, Judah preferred another way—its own—and ultimately lost its place with God.

1. Understanding God's Provisions

What was true in the days of Isaiah is equally true today—God has made provision for His people, yet, that provision is often overlooked or ignored. God spoke through Hosea to Israel, **"My people are destroyed for lack of knowledge" (Hosea 4:6).** Some of the Israelites were ignorant because they rejected God's knowledge. Others were not aware of God's provision because the teachers had not taught them about the benefits of God's covenant.

Crackers or Caviar?

I heard the story once of a poor immigrant who, for years, saved his money to come to America on a ship. After purchasing the ticket, he only had money left over for cheese and crackers to eat during the voyage. During the week-long trip, he often watched the other passengers in the dining rooms enjoying the sumptuous meals. On the day the ship docked in New York, one of the officers spoke to the man.

"Sir, are you okay?"

"Yes, fine," the man answered.

"Well, the ship's crew thought you might be ill since you didn't eat any meals with us," the officer said.

"Oh, no," the man replied, shaking his head. "I didn't have enough money to eat in the dining rooms… I only had money to pay for my ticket."

The officer looked at the man in disbelief. "Sir, I'm so sorry you didn't know—your meals were included in the price of your ticket."

Unfortunately, many of God's people are in the same boat as the immigrant sustaining himself on bread and cheese, while the Lord has made other, generous provision.

Of course there are sacrifices required of the disciple of the Lord, and we should be willing to suffer for Jesus when He calls us to take up our cross and follow Him. But some have taken that to mean we must not expect any special privileges as sons and daughters of the God of abundance. *It is vital for God's children to understand the provisions and benefits of the New Covenant.*

Without question, many of God's people remain ignorant of the benefits of Calvary. We continue to approach the Lord like beggars on the street when the Lord has declared us to be His children. Jesus encouraged his disciples to ask for good things from the Father and to expect to receive them:

If you hardhearted, sinful men know how to give good gifts to your children, won't your Father in heaven even more certainly give good gifts to those who ask him for them? (Matthew 7:11 TLB).

Prodigal Son or Elder Brother?

The story of the prodigal son in Luke 15 is a character type of a believer who understands the wealth of the Father. He sees the promise of the wealth, seeks for it and obtains it. The problem with the prodigal is that he wants to enjoy the treasures given to him without staying in the presence of the Father.

On the other hand, the elder brother is a character type of a believer who remains ignorant of his Father's provisions.

He never claims any financial or physical blessings. Rather, he slaves day after day in his Father's fields unaware that he, at any time, could ask his daddy for a lamb from the flocks to have a banquet with his friends. He remembers some of what the Father said to his family, but he decides these benefits are for another dispensation—a former one or a future one—rather than for present-day sons of the Father. In his theology, God is "The Great I Was" or "The Great I Will Be" rather than "The Great I Am."

Neither of these sons are good examples of the correct approach to the provisions of the Lord. God gave us all things to enjoy (I Timothy 6:17) in His presence and for His glory. As long as we seek first the kingdom of God and His right-eousness, all **"these things"** are added to us to enjoy, but not to abuse (Matthew 6:33). Let us read the New Will (Testament) and know without doubt what is ours in Christ.

2. Knowing the Word of God

Moses had died leaving Joshua as Senior Pastor of a very large congregation. Up until then he could rely on Moses to be responsible for major oversight of the flock and its host of associate pastors. Joshua faced a considerable confidence crisis. These people were accustomed to a pastor who had seen God face to face and who had received fresh revelations continuously. He must have been asking himself: "What will be the expectations of the people? How can I fill the shoes of a mighty man like Moses?" Then God spoke:

> **Moses My servant is dead; now therefore arise, cross this Jordan, you and all this people...**

No man will be able to stand before you all the days of your life. Just as I have been with Moses, I will be with you; I will not fail you or forsake you (Joshua 1:2,5 NASB).

Almost unbelievable! God would be with him as with Moses. But the Lord then instructed Joshua on how to be strong and confident for the ministry given to him: **"This book of the law shall not depart from your mouth, but you shall meditate on it day and night…" (Joshua 1:8 NASB).**

God's Word was to be the main source of Joshua's confidence. Just as Joshua, none of us can be full of courage and confidence for long if we neglect to meditate on the Holy Scriptures. This is not just memorizing Bible verses in order to quote them. We could cite every verse in the Bible and not really know the God of the Bible. Meditation is more than memorization. It is reading the Word, either aloud or silently, and allowing the Holy Spirit to speak the revelation of God's message to our minds and to our spirits. It is deep continued thought on a verse or passage of the Bible until it becomes a part of our thought patterns. In this way the word becomes more than just a collection of mental concepts—it becomes the essence of who we are.

When Jesus was tempted of the Devil, He was quick to report the source of His confidence by quoting from Deuteronomy: **"… man does not live on bread alone, but on every word that comes from the mouth of God" (Matthew 4:4 NIV).** Jesus was more concerned with what His Father was telling Him than in feeding His legitimate body appetites. He was living by the promptings of the Word of God. His victory over the enemy came because He knew the Word and was quick to say: **"It is written..." (Matthew 4:4,7,10).**

The Living Word

The Word of God testifies of its own life and power in Hebrews 4:12-13a (NASB):

> **For the word of God is living and active and sharper than any two-edged sword, and piercing as far as the division of soul and spirit, of both joints and marrow, and able to judge the thoughts and intentions of the heart.**
>
> **And there is no creature hidden from His sight...**

The Word presented in these verses is personified and made to be the Lord Himself. When we realize that God is in His Word, we cease simply studying the Word in an academic way and feed upon it until our spirits are filled with confidence in the Lord Himself. John tells us:

> **In the beginning was the Word and the Word was with God, and the Word was God...And the Word became flesh, and dwelt among us, and we beheld His glory, glory as of the only begotten from the Father, full of grace and truth (John 1:1,14 NASB).**

These verses cannot be fully understood by finite minds, but we know they tell us that to get more of the eternal logos (Word) in our hearts is to have more of the Lord Himself. That is why Paul admonishes us to **"Let the word of Christ richly dwell within you..." (Colossians 3:16a NASB).**

The strength of God and His Word is further conveyed in Hebrews 13:5-6:

Let your character be free from the love of money, being content with what you have; for He Himself has said, "I will never desert you, nor will I ever forsake you,"

So that we *confidently* say, "The Lord is my helper, I will not be afraid…"(NASB).

This is one of five Scripture promises from the original Greek in what is commonly referred to as a double negative before the verb. The original language reads "… **He Himself has said, I will not, I will not, cease to uphold and sustain thee."** The thought conveyed here is, no matter what problems life may bring, God will be there—leading, guiding, and bringing the believer into victory. The Lord Jesus will fight the battle and win the conflict for those who dare to trust in His Word. This is scriptural confidence. The Amplified Bible translates Hebrews 13:5, in the following manner:

…For He (God) Himself has said, "I will not in any way fail you nor give you up nor leave you without support. [I will] not, [I will] not, [I will] not in any degree leave you helpless, nor forsake nor let [you] down, [relax My hold on you]—Assuredly not!"

The Bible says about itself, that it is a **"sure word of prophecy" (II Peter 1:19)**. Thus, we can depend upon this Word when the world is shaking, and when the kingdoms of this earth are disintegrating.

3. Having Communion with God

Another vital source of confidence is found in maintaining a life of prayer and communication with the Lord. I Samuel 3:1 speaks about a peculiar time in the life of Israel, "… **when the word of the Lord was rare in those days: there was no widespread** *revelation*" **(NKJV)**.

One reason for this lack of vision or revelation was because the chief priest's sons, Hophni and Phinehas, were living in open sin. Their father Eli knew of his sons' sin, but failed to restrain them. They had actually made "… **the Lord's people to transgress" (I Samuel 2:24)**. Thus, sin was blocking God from speaking to the whole nation. When He did begin to speak through the lad, Samuel, God told him of the impending judgment upon Eli and his household because of their sins.

It is a terrible situation when the chief priest cannot hear the voice of God because he has allowed sin in his own house. The Lord was then forced to speak through the boy Samuel. God's chosen vessels have always been men and women who had the ability to communicate with and hear from the Almighty. Elijah, a man with passions like you and I, was one such instrument of God.

We are first introduced to Elijah in I Kings 17:1 when he walks boldly into an ungodly king's palace and brings the word of the Lord to the wicked ruler of Israel:

As the Lord God of Israel liveth, before whom I stand, there shall not be dew nor rain these years, but according to my word.

For sure, it takes confidence to enter a king's throne room without an invitation. But where did Elijah get this kind of confidence before kings? James 5:17-18 (NASB) fills us in on what happened prior to Elijah's courageous prophecy to Ahab:

> **Elijah was a man with a nature like ours, and he prayed earnestly that it might not rain; and it did not rain on the earth for three years and six months.**
>
> **And he prayed again, and the sky poured rain, and the earth produced its fruit.**

Elijah prayed until he knew he had the keys to the heavens. When he walked into the palace, he knew God had spoken to him and given him authority to speak His word concerning judgment on the nation of Israel. There would simply be no rain in the nation until the man of God prayed again for open heavens. And his words came to pass.

When present day prophets, recognized by the church, hear specific words from the Lord regarding our authority over public affairs, and then confidently speak prophetically regarding them, God will get the attention of our national leaders. Hearing from God is a prerequisite to walking in spiritual authority.

Pioneer Confidence

In the early days of the Charismatic Renewal, shortly after I received the Baptism in the Holy Spirit, I felt God nudging me to begin a new church in Pensacola, Florida. It seemed strange to me that God wanted another church in our city.

There were already numerous full gospel churches in the area. Besides, I felt the task was so awesome, and I had no confidence to begin.

Then, one night while preaching in Panama City, Florida, God spoke to me through prophecy. "My son," the prophecy began, "be not afraid to begin a work in your city for I have many people in your city who are hungry for Me." The person who spoke the prophecy did not know me, and I had told no one of my prompting about pioneering a work for the Lord. But the Lord had heard me when I prayed: "Lord, if this is really Your will for me to begin a church, please let me know." When God answered I was able to move forward with great confidence. The greatest confidence that we can have is knowing that we are in the will of God. This should be our continual quest.

I came back to Pensacola and rented a little storefront building with full confidence that God was going to grant me the wisdom and favor to plant Liberty Church in our city. Time has proven that God definitely wanted another community of believers in Pensacola, but it was this prophetic word that kept me going in the early days when everything seemed to be against our little group meeting in a storefront. In my heart, I knew God had spoken and would grant us favor in spite of the gainsayers and scoffers who publicly ridiculed our people as flakes and heretics. The Lord answered our prayers and gave us confidence to be witnesses rather than lawyers. We simply witnessed to what God had done for us and did not argue with our adversaries. Satan cannot stop anyone who knows God is directing and ordering his steps.

4. Remembering Past Victories

For many years as a young boy I sang with other church worshippers "Here I raise mine Ebenezer" from Charles Wesley's song *Come Thou Fount*, but I did not know what it meant. I later learned that the word "Ebenezer" is taken from I Samuel 7:12 and means: "Hitherto hath the Lord helped us." It was the name of a stone set up by Samuel to help Israel remember how the Lord had helped them in the battles against the Philistines.

It is important that we remember God's past blessings in our lives. Even though you faced trouble in the past, remember how God kept His promises in the midst of all your battles. Call those victories to mind if you wish to truly produce renewed confidence in your life. They are testimonies of God's faithfulness.

Psalm 78 recalls the story of how God's people forgot all the great things He had done on their behalf:

For He established a testimony in Jacob, and appointed a law in Israel, which he commanded our fathers, that they should make them known to their children:

That they might set their hope in God, and not forget the works of God, but keep his commandments:

They kept not the covenant of God, and refused to walk in his law; and forgat his works, and his wonders that he had shown them.

> **Yea, they turned back and tempted God, and limited the Holy One of Israel.**
>
> **They remembered not his hand, nor the day when he delivered them from the enemy.**
>
> **Yet they tempted and provoked the most high God, and kept not his testimonies:**
>
> **But turned back, and dealt unfaithfully like their fathers: they were turned aside like a deceitful bow (verses 5,7,10,11,41,42,56,57).**

Many of the Psalms are actually affirmations of the past faithfulness of God to the Psalmist who had faced difficulty and trouble in his daily life. We are reminded by Revelation 12:11 that **"... the word of their testimony"** is one way in which the believer overcomes Satan's accusations and attacks. Thus, our testimony of God's faithfulness is absolutely vital if we are to walk every day in confidence.

5. Seeing Others Stand

Our lifestyle of faith in God can also be a source of confidence to others. In the case of the apostle Paul, he sees favorable results in his own imprisonment, according to Philippians 1:12-14:

> **But I would ye should understand, brethren, that the things which happened unto me have fallen out rather unto the furtherance of the gospel;**

So that my bonds in Christ are manifest in all the palace, and in all other places;

And many of the brethren in the Lord, waxing confident by my bonds, are much more bold to speak the word without fear.

Paul is saying that others have become bold in their faith from having seen him stand during times of severe persecution. This produced strength and endurance in his companions · who admired the apostle's steadfast tenacity and commitment to his calling. According to Paul's own testimony, he was impacted by Stephen's stand for the Lord, particularly the way in which he willingly and courageously became the first martyr for Jesus. Many Bible teachers contend that Paul's role in Stephen's death caused him much inward pain and prepared him for a visitation from the Lord.

Roger Bannister, a British athlete, became the first man to run a mile in less than four minutes. He ran a mile in 3 minutes and 59.4 seconds at Oxford, England on May 6, 1954. Only one month later his record was broken by John Landy, an Australian. In August of the same year, Bannister defeated Landy by running the mile in 3 minutes 58.8 seconds. Since then it has been broken several times. The only valid explanation for this sudden progress in the sport is that the runners experienced an explosion of confidence which enabled them to break the world record while winning the race.

In this same way, a breakthrough experienced by one of the brethren can encourage many others to press beyond their previous limitations. If each of us were able to concentrate until we experienced a breakthrough, soon the entire body of Christ would be experiencing a major advance. Each victory encourages other victories until we all attain the ultimate victory.

We can all bring to mind those who are our heroes of faith and perseverance. Rather than focusing on failures and negative reports, we can call to remembrance those who have stood fast and strong, whether it be Bible characters or contemporary champions of courage and forbearance.

Other people are watching our life in Christ. We are an example of God's faithfulness and we can build morale in our friends when we remain faithful in times of testing. While that should not be the only criteria for standing in faith, it is certainly a worthwhile consideration.

6. Taking a Stand

Throughout the pages of the Bible, many wonderful stories are recounted. Few are told more vividly than those told about David or written by him. It seems this man knew firsthand the constant risks of being a leader appointed by God. Listen to his words, declaring his relationship with the Lord:

The Lord is my light and my salvation; whom shall I fear? the Lord is the strength of my life; of whom shall I be afraid?

When the wicked, even mine enemies and my foes, came upon me to eat up my flesh, they stumbled and fell.

Though an host should encamp against me, my heart shall not fear: though war should rise against me, in this *will I be confident* **(Psalm 27:1-3).**

Sometimes, it seems, we simply have to make up our minds that we are going to live confidently in God. This means standing up on the inside, determining to be optimistic, regardless of the circumstances.

No doubt that's what David did when his enemies seemed to have the upper hand. His life was filled with incredible ups and downs—perhaps more than that of the average person.

Paul tells us: **"... having done all, to stand" (Ephesians 6:13)**. Occasionally you will know of nothing else to do during a furious spiritual battle. It is then, more than any other time, you must make up your mind to stand and believe that all is well.

Possess What God Has Given

The Scriptures teach that, even though God has given us something, we must often fight to possess it, just as Israel had to fight against the Canaanites, Perizites, Hittites to possess their promised land. The Lord could have done all of the fighting for Israel, just as He could for us, but obviously He has something else in mind. He wants us to learn how to fight! He allows opposition in our lives for our sakes. He often allows the enemy to oppose us in receiving that which He has promised. This fact is illustrated from Genesis to Revelation. For this reason all of His promises to the seven churches in Revelation were to the "overcomers."

Paul wrote to his spiritual son, Timothy: **"God has not given us the spirit of fear [timidity], but of power, and of love and a sound mind" (II Timothy 1:7).** Evidently the young disciple had drawn back from speaking out for Jesus because of opposition. He had to be reminded that his timidity was not from the Lord. Many draw back, intimidated by the opposition, and do not possess what God has called them to occupy. Joshua wrestled with intimidation; and the Lord's instructions for him included encouragement, which we also should heed:

> **Be strong and of a good courage: for unto this people shalt thou divide for an inheritance the land, which I sware unto their fathers to give them.**

> **Only be thou strong and very courageous, that thou mayest observe to do according to all the law, which Moses my servant commanded thee: turn not from it to the right hand or to the left, that thou mayest prosper whithersoever thou goest.**

> **Have not I commanded thee? be strong and of a good courage; be not afraid, neither be thou dismayed: for the Lord thy God is with thee whithersoever thou goest (Joshua 1:6-7, 9).**

Taking courage in God's promises, Joshua stood up on the inside; he divided the land of Canaan among the tribes of Israel even before he crossed the Jordan. He was fully convinced that God was with him and would give him success in occupying the promised land.

7. Being Filled with the Holy Spirit

Finally, the greatest way for us to develop confidence is to be filled continually with the Holy Spirit. We see this repeatedly in the Book of Acts. Not only were the disciples baptized in the Holy Spirit on the day of Pentecost; they were refilled with the Spirit while praying together later during strong persecution in Jerusalem:

And when they had prayed, the place where they had gathered was shaken, and they were all filled with the Holy Spirit, and began to speak the word of God with boldness (Acts 4:31 NASB).

Paul tells us to: "**... be filled with the Spirit, speaking to one another in psalms and hymns and spiritual songs, singing and making melody with your heart to the Lord" (Ephesians 5:18b-19, NASB).** Not only are we told to keep on being filled with the Holy Spirit, but we are given the means by which we can stay filled—through continued singing to one another and to the Lord with psalms, hymns and spiritual songs.

Jude confirms the need to keep speaking in the spirit: **"But you, beloved, building yourselves up on your most holy faith; praying in the Holy Spirit" (Jude 20 NASB).** Speaking in tongues is not just an evidence of the Baptism in the Holy Spirit; it is a tool by which we can communicate with the Lord in the Spirit, strengthening our own faith.

Paul corrected the Corinthian church because of their abuse of tongues, especially those who spoke out in the congregation with no interpretation of the message. He said it was distracting and confusing to those who did not understand what was happening. However, he also said that he himself spoke in other tongues more than all the Corinthians (I Corinthians 14:18), explaining that a person who speaks in tongues privately builds up his own faith. Thus, his reason is clear—he prayed in the Spirit often to increase his confidence in the Lord and in his calling.

There is nothing on earth to equal the working of the Holy Spirit in a person's life. Before Pentecost, Peter was not confident enough to stand up to servant girls in a courtyard where the enemies of Jesus had brought Him for trial. Even after he witnessed the resurrection of Jesus, he was so discouraged, he returned to his old occupation. It was only after Jesus poured out the Holy Spirit on the day of Pentecost that Peter preached with holy boldness, resulting in three thousand conversions on that one day.

The Scriptures teach that the Holy Spirit has come to earth to administrate the affairs of the Lord until He returns. His role includes transforming believers into confident witnesses of Jesus, and giving comfort and guidance to those who submit to His Lordship. So let us obey the Lord's command: **"Be filled with the Holy Spirit" (Ephesians 5:18b).**

Chapter Four

Confidence: Birthed in Righteousness

The wicked flee when no one is pursuing, but the righteous are bold (confident) as a lion (Proverbs 28:1 NASB).

All genuine confidence begins with a right relationship with God. David understood this great truth and declared: **"The Lord is my light and my salvation... in this will I be confident" (Psalm 27:1,3)**. His confidence was founded in his trust in the living God for his righteousness.

When Adam sinned, his whole nature, and that of all future descendants was corrupted. This is what theologians call "original sin," and is an essential truth which must be acknowledged by every person. Paul explains this:

When Adam sinned, sin entered the entire human race. His sin spread death throughout all the

world, so everything began to grow old and die...The sin of this one man, Adam, caused death to be king *over all*... **(Romans 5:12,17a, TLB).**

The first words Adam spoke after his fall were: **"I heard thy voice in the garden, and I was afraid, because I was naked; and I hid myself," (Genesis 3:10).** He had lost his confidence in the presence of God because he had transgressed. A man may convince himself that he can find peace and confidence without the righteousness of God, but he never really can. An emptiness resides in the heart of every person until He repents and becomes rightly related to God.

The Book of Righteousness

The book of Romans is called the book of righteousness. The author, Paul, first establishes the foundational truth that **"there is none righteous, no, not one," (Romans 3:10).** He then speaks of his own family, the Israelites, and the futility of their own way:

I know what enthusiasm they have for the honor of God, but it is misdirected zeal.

For they don't understand that Christ has died to make them right with God. Instead they are trying to make themselves good enough to gain God's favor by keeping the Jewish laws and customs, but that is not God's way of salvation....

For salvation that comes from trusting Christ... is already within easy reach of each of us; in fact, it is as near as our own hearts and mouths. For if you tell others with your own mouth that Jesus

Christ is your Lord, and believe in your own heart that God has raised Him from the dead, you will be saved.

For it is by believing in his heart that a man becomes right with God; and with his mouth he tells others of his faith, confirming his salvation, (Romans 10:2-3,8-10 TLB).

The Law Brings Us to Jesus

The Law is not able to save; it can only lead us to Christ who can save us. Paul tells us that the Law is good, but it is only a schoolmaster to bring us to Christ. It reveals our guilt and shows us our need for the Savior.

But why talk about guilt when we are attempting to build confidence? Doesn't guilt destroy confidence? It does, but no person can receive genuine Bible-based confidence until he loses confidence in his own ability to do that which is right. Furthermore, he must lose dependence on his own resources for self-assurance. Self-assurance is a counterfeit for the true confidence that only comes from knowing deep within our hearts that we are right with God.

Some choose alcohol, drugs, or even karate in order to feel confident and secure, but these will never substitute for true confidence. Hospitals, psychiatric wards, and prisons can clearly attest to this. True confidence can only have one source—God. He made us, and He alone can remake us into who we are called to be. The Lord does not impute righteousness to anyone until we are convicted of sin by the Holy Spirit. Only then will we be truly open to receive God's gift of righteousness in the Lord Jesus Christ. The confidence we can then have in His provision surpasses anything that we can have in ourselves.

Paul looked at his own heart and declared: **"O wretched man that I am! who shall deliver me from the body of this death?" (Romans 7:24).** The answer he gave is the only true answer to the dilemma of overwhelming guilt. He exclaimed: **"I thank God through Jesus Christ our Lord... There is therefore now no condemnation to them which are in Christ Jesus" (Romans 8:1).** Only Jesus could relieve the pain of Paul's troubled soul. Absolutely nothing but the blood of Jesus can purge our conscience from evil works and give us assurance that we have been made right with God.

> **But all these things that I once thought very worthwhile—now I've thrown them all away so that I can put my trust and hope *in Christ alone* (Philippians 3:7 TLB).**

Gloria Swanson's Guilt

Gloria Swanson tells of her battle with guilt in her best-selling autobiography, *Swanson on Swanson.* The book repeats again and again her remorse over taking her unborn baby's life when she was 25 years old. In spite of her great fame, she could not forget what she had done 55 years earlier.

In the book's introduction, she states: "I am going to start with a moment in my life when I was never happier. I was 25 and the most popular celebrity in the world. What nobody knew was that I was pregnant. Even the father of the child did not know about it" She knew if she had a child in seven months, her career would be finished. She consulted a friend who arranged for her to have an abortion. The doctor botched the operation and for weeks she lay at the point of death in a Paris hospital. Night after night she would have nightmares about "the child I had killed."

After attending a premier of one of her famous films, she remembers a conversation with her mother who said: "Gloria, this should be the happiest night of your life." She replied: "No, mother, it is the saddest." Explaining her answer, she writes that, at that point in her life, she was thinking of the price she had paid to be able to celebrate and walk the orchid strewn aisle. She recalled a conversation with her friend who prepared her for the abortion. The voice of the doctor haunted her mind: "Everything is all right." But the clearest voice in her memory was that of her unborn child. "Don't do it" the voice had said. "Don't do it. I know you hear me. Listen to me! I want to live! I'm frightened of the sewer." According to the autobiography, Gloria's greatest regret was that she had not given birth to that baby. She says: "Nothing in the whole world is worth a baby. I realized it too late and have never stopped blaming myself."[1]

Her guilt was real and can never be rationalized away—but it can be cleansed away! Through Jesus we can be forgiven and even have our conscience cleansed. Sin does condemn us in our hearts, and those who do not find salvation through the sacrifice of Jesus will look for relief in the wrong places, and those wrong places will always ultimately lead to more guilt. Regardless of the facades men may wear, confidence and peace cannot be truly found except through faith in the Lord Jesus Christ.

Swanson moved temporarily to the Far East looking for relief in Hinduism and other Eastern religions. Others scour the earth looking for it. Paul, who had been a religious bigot, persecutor, and murderer of the followers of Jesus, understood this very well. He is one of the great testimonies of God's grace and forgiveness. That forgiveness gave him such a peace and confidence that the officials of the greatest Empire cowered as he entered their cities. Paul's confidence is evident:

I am persuaded that neither death, nor life, nor angels, nor principalities, nor things present, nor things to come, nor powers, nor shall height, nor depth, nor any other creature,

be able to separate us from the love of God, which is in Christ Jesus our Lord (Romans 8:38-39 ASV).

Condemnation Kills Confidence

For God sent not his Son into the world to condemn the world; but that the world through him might be saved (John 3:17).

I am ashamed of myself when I think of the early days of my ministry and how I tried to promote holiness, but condemned a lot of good people in the process. A woman once said kindly to me: "Brother Ken, I come to church feeling pretty good, but when I leave I feel like a whipped dog." Of course, I was hurt deep inside by such a statement because I didn't intend to cause her harm. However, I felt I needed to provoke people if they were going to change for the better and walk in holiness. But does this promote true conviction?

My ideas of holiness were sincere; I never enjoyed vocally bashing people. I preached against "short-shorts", alcohol, movies, apathy, compromise, and anything else that wasn't on my list of legitimate activities. I still believe that ministers need to cry out against sin. In fact, Isaiah said, **"Cry aloud and spare not, lift up thy voice like a trumpet, and shew my people their transgression..."** **(Isaiah 58:1).** There is a place for tough preaching against sin, but it must always lead to our deliverance from sin through the cross. The Law is good as a schoolmaster to bring men to Christ, but the preaching of the Law alone will not empower them to obey it:

> **For what the law could not do, in that it was weak because of the flesh, God sending His own Son in the likeness of sinful flesh, and for sin, condemned sin in the flesh: that the righteousness of the law might be fulfilled in us who walk not after the flesh, but after the Spirit (Romans 8:3-5).**

The true ministry of reconciliation builds confidence in God and empowers people to overcome sin. Most churches are filled with people who are already under condemnation. It is true that many are also walking outside the fear of the Lord and need to hear of the consequences of sin. However, the preaching of Christ and His desire and power to give forgiveness and resurrection life to each believer should be the priority of every minister of the Word.

Satan makes every effort to cause Christians to feel less than righteous. His primary occupation is to accuse the children of God day and night. Our victory over him comes when we apply the Blood of Jesus to the lintels and doorposts of our minds and hearts.

A young married man came to me recently with a serious problem with pornography. His conscience was hurting badly, and he feared rejection from his wife and friends over discovery of his problems. After all, he was a respected church member and a leader in his church.

My inclination was not to make him feel any worse than he already did. I certainly could not condone his pornographic magazines or his slipping into nightclubs to watch strippers. But he already knew the wretchedness of his sin; what he needed was to know how to overcome this terrible temptation and bondage to lust. Had he not already felt the conviction it may have been appropriate to "preach" against his sins, but what he needed now was not more conviction but the power of the cross to overcome his sin. He also needed the fellowship of others who had fought the same battle and been victorious, and who would stand by him as he learned to stand in the victory of the cross. By God's grace, we can **"cleanse ourselves from all filthiness of the flesh and spirit, perfecting holiness in the fear of God" (II Corinthians 7:1).** Then we can walk in peace and assurance and be as **"bold as a lion" (Proverbs 28:1 NASB).**

Watch Out for Counterfeit Confidence

New Agers—who represent a wedding of the philosophies of Hinduism, Buddhism, Astrology and the Occult—have infiltrated most every segment of society, particularly education, religion, the news media, and the motion picture industry. One foundation of New Age Philosophy is a humanistically based psychology.

Their focus is upon love, forgiveness and human rights. Their message sounds much like Christian truth, yet their agenda is dramatically different than the Christian's purpose. Though they sincerely seek for social justice and equity in business, labor and government, they do not accept the same moral values as Bible-believing Christians do. They even use Christ as a model but recognize Him as God only in the sense they see everyone else as gods. In their view, Jesus simply had developed further than others in His journey to deity.

In some instances, they embrace the doctrine of reincarnation which has gained an increasing number of converts since the publication of Shirley MacLaine's book, *Out on a Limb.* Because of the great hunger for the supernatural, over two million copies of this book have been sold. In a 12-page color supplement in the Los Angeles *Times,* followers of Hare Krishna stated: *"Reincarnation is fast becoming the most popular explanation for the afterlife...A recent Gallup poll in America showed that over 30% of people under 30 accept reincarnation as an explanation of life after death."*[2]

These figures are likely an exaggeration, but even if they are true, it means 70% of people under 30 do not believe in reincarnation. It also means New Agers are going after the minds of the younger generation. In order to believe in reincarnation, the Bible must be rejected as the Word of God. It is absolutely impossible to accept the Bible as the infallible Word of God and also accept the belief in returning to the earth as another person. Hebrews 9:27 (ASV) explicitly states: **"It is appointed unto man once to die and after this cometh judgment."**

False Sources of Confidence

My purpose in sounding this alarm against counterfeit confidence is to prevent hurting and spiritually hungry people from false sources of confidence. Our main goal should not be confidence, but rather a right standing before God which will result in a true confidence. The apostle Paul tells us:

Beware of dogs, beware of evil workers, beware of circumcision. For we are the circumcision, which worship God in the spirit and rejoice in Christ Jesus, and have no confidence in the flesh (Philippians 3:2 ASV).

But I fear, lest by any means as the serpent beguiled Eve through his craftiness your minds should be corrupted from the simplicity and the purity that is toward Christ (II Corinthians 11:3).

Isaiah made it clear that God has prepared a sure foundation and laid a precious cornerstone and those who believe on Him should never be ashamed. He is our refuge, and waters of judgment shall:

Sweep away the refuge of lies and the waters shall overflow the (imitation) hiding place and your covenant with death shall be disannulled, and your agreement with hell shall not stand...for the bed is shorter than that a man can stretch himself on it; and the covering narrower than that he can wrap himself in it (Isaiah 28:17,18,20).

Any attempt to find refuge or eternal life in any source other than the Lord Himself is like trying to sleep under very narrow covers on a very short bed. It leaves the seeker exposed and uncovered at the day of accounting.

The Supernatural Is Essential

Paul McGuire a respected film producer and former new ager wrote:

> The only reason the New Age movement has become a significant force in our world is because it rushed in to fill the spiritual void left by a Church that denied the reality of the supernatural and turned its back on the teachings of Christ Who commanded His people to be "clothed with power from on high" and to "proclaim the gospel of the kingdom." As I was growing up in New York City, I literally hated the church…and became involved in N.A.M. I was seduced and brainwashed to believe that there are many ways to heaven and that there is no such thing as evil incarnate or a devil.[3]

We must once again wait in prayer until we are clothed with power from on high. It is in a supernatural atmosphere that individuals like Paul McGuire are deceived. Men were created to have fellowship with God who is Spirit; therefore they have a void in their life for the supernatural. If this void is not filled with the supernatural power of God, it will be filled by the evil one. Christianity was supernatural from its very first day, and it will be supernatural until the last. The Lord gave His church supernatural power to be witnesses of His resurrection, and the world will require no less in order to really believe it.

Summary

He made him who knew (experienced) no sin to be sin on our behalf, that we might become the righteousness of God in Him (II Corinthians 5:21 NASB).

Righteousness has been wonderfully described in the inspiring poem, *The Perfect Righteousness of God,* by Albert Midland.

> *The Perfect righteousness of God*
> *Is witnessed in the Savior's blood*
> *'Tis in the cross of Christ we trace*
> *His righteousness, yet wondrous grace.*
> *God could not pass the sinner by,*
> *His sin demands that he must die;*
> *But in the cross of Christ we see*
> *How God can save, yet righteous be.*
> *The sin alights in Jesus' head,*
> *'Tis in His blood sin's debt is paid;*
> *Stern Justice can demand no more,*
> *And Mercy can dispense her store.*
> *The sinner who believes is free,*
> *Can say, "The Savior died for me;"*
> *Can point to the atoning blood,*
> *And say, "This made my peace with God." [4]*

Surely, inward righteousness, or a right standing with God, is an important key to walking in confidence. We must be regenerated inwardly by faith and then walk it outwardly by faith.

For what the law could not do, in that it was weak through the flesh, God sending His own Son in the likeness of sinful flesh, and for sin, condemned sin in the flesh:

that the righteousness of the law might be fulfilled in us, who walk not after the flesh, but after the Spirit (Romans 8:3,4).

In His redemptive plan, God has dealt directly with only two men—Adam and Christ. All his subsequent dealings with the human race hinge on His considerations of these two men. I Corinthians 15:21-22 and Romans 5:17 confirm this singular truth:

> **For inasmuch as death came through a man, the resurrection from the dead is also through a man.**

> **For just as in Adam all die, so in Christ shall all be made alive (I Corinthians 15:21-22).**

> **For if by the transgression of the one, death reigned through the one, much more those who receive the abundance of grace and of the gift of righteousness will reign in life through the One, Jesus Christ (Romans 5:17, NASB).**

We inherited death from Adam, and as long as we are in Adam, death reigns in us. We must be transferred from our position "in Adam" to a position "in Christ" to satisfy God. Jesus Christ alone can exchange sin and death for righteousness and resurrection life. Confidence is birthed in the righteousness of Christ.

Chapter Five

The Patriarchs of Confidence

Throughout recorded history men and women of faith have overcome formidable obstacles to serve the living God. In Hebrews 12, these patriarchs are called "a great cloud of witnesses":

> **Wherefore seeing we also are compassed about with so great a cloud of witnesses, let us lay aside every weight, and the sin which doth so easily beset us, and let us run with patience the race that is set before us,**
>
> **Looking unto Jesus the author and finisher of our faith; who for the joy that was set before him endured the cross, despising the shame, and is set down at the right hand of the *throne of God* (Hebrews 12:1-2).**

As God's people of the New Covenant, we are encompassed about with this great cloud of Old Covenant witnesses, some of which are listed in Hebrews 11 — Abel, Enoch, Noah, Abraham, Sarah, Isaac, Jacob, Joseph, Moses, Rahab, Gideon, Barak, Samson, Jephthah, David, Samuel and the prophets. Their lives are witnesses to encourage us to finish the course which they began, to fully accomplish the purpose of God for our own generation.

The Trials of Our Faith

When confronted with someone in the midst of a trying, fiery test, I've heard people say, "Oh, that's so strange. That's so unusual for God to allow me to be treated that way." It is not unusual, or strange. It is God's way which the Scripture clearly teaches:

Beloved, think it not strange concerning the fiery trial which is to try you, as though some strange thing happened unto you (I Peter 4:12).

Let us take a brief look at some of the heroes of the faith listed in Hebrews 11 as examples of how confidence worked with their faith in the midst of severe trials.

Enoch

Enoch walked with God and **"was not found for God had translated him" (Hebrews 11:5).** Enoch communed daily with the Lord, and one day God just took him to heaven. Andrew Bonar suggests that God and Enoch were in the habit of taking a long walk together each day, and one day God said to Enoch: "Why go home? Come all the way with me." It is as if Enoch got so close to God that he just could not stay on earth any longer. So at 365 years of age, he went to Heaven without having to die. Only two men of the Bible never died—Enoch and Elijah. They were caught up to heaven just as Christians will be who are alive when Christ returns to earth.

I used to visualize Enoch just spending each day with the Lord Himself. But that's not what the Bible says. It says Enoch "walked" with God, which I now believe means he just lived his everyday life, doing the same everyday routine things you and I do, but always with God. The word "walk" as used in the Bible gives us insight into this. For example:

> **They that wait upon the Lord...shall mount up with wings like eagles, they will run and not get tired, they will *walk* and not become weary (Isaiah 40:31 NASB).**

Figuratively, walking signifies the whole round of activities or conduct in a person's life. Walking is something that we do almost unconsciously, which is the way that we also tend to carry out many of life's activities and duties. Because Enoch included the Lord in all of his activities, they were transformed from the dull and mundane and were given purpose and meaning.

The Scriptures exhort us to do **"everything as unto the Lord" (Col 3:23).** Everything that we do should be worship. This can transform even the most mundane task into a glorious encounter with heaven. In a sense, we too can be translated from the ordinary and mundane to the glory of heaven, in even our most simple tasks, simply by including the Lord in them. As Elizabeth Barrett Browning eloquently said, "Earth is crammed with heaven. Every bush is aflame with the fire of God, but only those who see take off their shoes. The rest just pick the berries."

Enoch is a wonderful testimony that even the most basic, simple task such as walking, can be transforming if we do it in fellowship with God.

Enoch lived in a corrupt time, and he spoke out boldly against the wicked and their destiny:

> **And about these also Enoch, in the seventh generation from Adam, prophesied, saying, Behold, the Lord came with many thousands of His holy ones,**
>
> **to execute judgment upon all, and to convict all the ungodly of all their ungodly deeds which they have done in an ungodly way, and of all the harsh things which ungodly sinners have spoken against Him (Jude 14,15 NASB).**

God was real to Enoch. For over 300 years, he communed with Him and received revelation concerning things to come in our own day. Before he was taken up, it was already recorded that pleased the Lord. That was his passion—to delight the Lord in all that he did.

There is no record that Enoch was trying to obtain more faith; he simply obeyed the Lord in everything and God called *that* faith. What better testimony can be written about anyone that this: "**...he was pleasing to God. And without faith it is impossible to please Him, for he that comes to God must** believe that He is, and that He is a rewarder of those who seek Him" (Hebrews 11:5b,6 NASB).

Enoch's reward was to be placed on the missing person's list—for God caught him up into His glory! Could there possibly be a better way to go? Is it not also probable that Enoch is a witness that the generation that is taken up at the coming of the Lord will have likewise found the secret of a transformed life—walking with God in all that they do?

Noah

Like Enoch, Noah was not seeking faith; he simply obeyed the Lord, and God called it faith. If things were corrupt in the days of Enoch, they were much more so when Noah lived. The account reads:

> **Then the Lord saw the wickedness of man was great on the earth, and that every intent of the thoughts of his heart was only evil continually...**
>
> **and the Lord said, "I will blot out man...for I am sorry that I have made them."**
>
> **But Noah found favor in the eyes of the Lord...Noah was a righteous man, blameless in his time; and Noah walked with God (Genesis 6:5, 7b,8,9 NASB).**

The story is also recorded in Hebrews 11:7:

> **By faith Noah, being warned of God of things not seen as yet, moved with fear, prepared an ark to the saving of his house; by the which he**

condemned the world, and became heir of the righteousness which is by faith.

Please note that Noah was not declared righteous because he built an ark. He built an ark because he had confidence in God. Because of his faith, acted out in obedience, he was declared righteous.

If you are a pastor and you have become frustrated with your congregation, consider Noah—he preached for 100 years to people who would not listen. If you have become discouraged with the lack of motivation in your building projects, consider Noah—he undertook the seemingly impossible task of building a boat when none had ever been seen before, and before the first drop of rain had fallen on the earth. Yet, without a Bible for encouragement, and without the testimony of others, Noah was persistent and steadfast. He completed his task. That is faith!

The word "steadfast" is derived from "steedfast" which refers to a warrior staying fast on his horse or steed during battle. This is one of the most powerful words used in the Bible in relation to our calling and purpose in God. In the clamor of battle just staying on the horse can be a feat. When we are given a task by God we must determine that we are not going to be knocked off by the opposition and discouragement that invariably comes. Noah is one of the great examples of the faith, steadfastness, and confidence which is required for those who undertake the commission of God.

It was Israel's lack of steadfastness that cost them victory time after time. Even when blessed with miracles on a daily basis, they complained. They were not steadfast in their trust of God when they could not see, feel, smell, touch or taste something tangible. Why? Because they walked by sight and not by faith in God. They did not trust in God's goodness, nor did they believe in His unfailing promises, nor did they continually hold their confidence in Him. In Psalm 78:8 they are described as: "... **a stubborn and rebellious generation; a generation that set not their heart aright, and whose spirit was not steadfast with God.**"

Noah also had his weaknesses as shown by his behavior after the flood. Everyone has bad days, but Noah kept his confidence in God, steadfastly believing that the Almighty had spoken the truth and would perform what He had promised. When God destroyed the unrighteous from the earth, Noah and his family were spared from the destruction—thereby sparing the whole human race from extinction. We should thank God for Noah, but we should also seek faith and confidence like his, so that we can accomplish God's purpose in our generation.

Abraham

Chosen of God, friend of God, father of the faithful, the first Hebrew, exalted father, father of nations—are all titles which were given to Abraham. Born in Ur of the Chaldees, Abraham was a Gentile from what is now Iraq, but the Lord chose him to be the father of a new spiritual race. Though also subject to failures and cowardly at times, his confidence in the Lord enabled him to obey God's command, and leave his home to travel into an unknown land to seek His purposes. As a result, Abraham received three promises from the Lord: (1) the land of Canaan for his descendants, (2) the promise of posterity, and (3) the promise of a spiritual seed (Christ) who would bless all the people on earth:

> **By faith, Abraham, when he was called, obeyed by going out to a place which he was to receive for an inheritance; and he went out, not knowing where he was going. By faith he lived as an alien in the land of promise, as in a foreign land, dwelling in tents with Isaac and Jacob, fellow heirs of the same promise;**
>
> **for he was looking for a city which has foundations, whose architect and builder is God (Hebrews 11:8-10 NASB).**

In the beginning of His encounters with Abraham, God did not reveal all that He had in mind. It seemed enough at first just to test Abraham's obedience and to get him away from Ur and his family. After several years, the Lord made a new covenant with Abraham and gave him the promise of a son:

> **And Abram said, "O Lord God, what wilt Thou give me, since I am childless"...**
>
> **Then behold, the word of the Lord came to him saying, "...one who shall come forth from your own body, he shall be your heir." And he took him outside and said, "Now look toward the heavens, and count the stars, if you are able to count them...So your descendants be."**
>
> **Then he believed in the Lord; and He reckoned it to him as righteousness (Genesis 15:2,4-6 NASB).**

At the time this covenant was made, Abraham was 75 years old and Sarah was 65, and barren. Yet, Abraham believed God. Of course, God did not say that the promised child would arrive after 25 years of waiting. The promise was so significant that it could only be fulfilled in God's way and in His timing. According to Paul, Abraham did not even consider the overwhelming impossibility of the promise:

In hope against hope, he believed,...

and without becoming weak in faith he contemplated his own body, now as good as dead since he was about a hundred years old, and the deadness of Sarah's womb;

yet, with respect to the promise of God, he did not waver in unbelief, but grew strong in faith, giving glory to God,

and being fully assured [confident] that what He had promised, He was able also to perform (Romans 4:18-21 NASB).

Notice these words: **"In hope against hope, he believed."** We might translate that to mean that when he quit having any hope in his own ability, he still hoped in God.

It is interesting that all of these great heroes of the faith had their confidence tried by a long passage of time. Time erodes pseudo faith, but purifies that which is true. Time gives us the opportunity to grow in faith, not waning, if we possess that which is real. Even so, Abraham's greatest test came after he had received his promise of a son, as is noted in Hebrews 11:17,19:

> **By faith, Abraham, when he was tested, offered up Isaac; and he who had received the promises was offering up his only begotten son;**
>
> **He considered that God was able to raise men even from the dead; from which he also received him back as a type (NASB).**

Abraham had proven his confidence in God's promise of his descendants coming through Isaac. In this test he had to trust God far beyond any reason or human possibility. He had to believe that even if he sacrificed Isaac, the Lord would raise him up again for the promise to be fulfilled.

God placed this great demand on Abraham's faith for two reasons: to determine how devoted Abraham was to him, and to illustrate the sacrifice and resurrection of Jesus through the type of Issac. Abraham's success in these crucial tests surely explains why He is called the father of the faithful and a friend of God.

Sarah

The poet Longfellow has written: *"As unto the bow the cord is, So unto the man the woman. Though she bends him, she obeys him, Though she draws him, yet she follows. Useless each without the other."* This is an excellent portrayal of the relationship of Abraham and Sarah.

Her name Sarai, meaning "Princess," shows she came from a noble family. According to the Bible, she was a beautiful woman, and many stories tell of her growing attractiveness through the years, even when she was very old. She too trusted in the faithfulness of God as she was the only wife of the heroes of faith who was mentioned in Hebrews 11.

God Himself changed her name from Sarai to Sarah. She was promoted from a princess to **"the mother of us all"** **(Galatians 4:26).** She is also called a "freewoman" in comparison to Hagar, the "bondwoman". Sarah loved her husband and called him "lord" (see I Peter 3:6), yet she was not a slave to Abraham, but his wife and co-laborer. It was through her own faith that she **"...received strength to conceive seed, and was delivered of a child when she was past age, because she judged him faithful who had promised"** **(Hebrews 11:11).** Through Sarah the Lord honors the faith of wives and mothers, which is no doubt essential to the bringing forth of the seed of the righteous, perpetuating the purposes of God on the earth.

Moses

Next to Abraham, Moses would be the man who was mentioned most as an instrument of God in His redemptive plan. This great Hebrew leader was born at the very time the Pharaoh of Egypt had resolved to destroy every newborn male child among the Israelites. The account of his early life—from his rescue in the river by Pharaoh's daughter to his royal upbringing—has enraptured the hearts of children for generations. It is the story of the purposes of God prevailing against the most powerful forces that the earth can muster to destroy them.

It would take volumes to fully expound the virtues of Moses as historian, leader, statesman, and patriot, but his greatest honor was to be the instrument of God to set His people free from the yoke of slavery. His life is an inspiration to all who are likewise called to be used as deliverers of those in bondage.

Five specific events stand out in the life of Moses:

(1) His initial turning to God with all his heart,

> **refusing to be called the son of Pharaoh's daughter, choosing rather to endure ill treatment with the people of God than to enjoy the passing pleasures of sin, considering the reproach of Christ greater riches than the treasures of Egypt...(Hebrews 11:24b-26 NASB).**

(2) His encounter with God in the wilderness when he was called to lead the children of Israel out of Egypt.

(3) His confrontations with Pharaoh for the release of God's people that resulted in their liberation.

(4) The revelation that God gave him of the blood atonment.

(5) The giving of the Law on Mount Sinai.

The Scriptures teach that because of Moses' confidence in God, he "left Egypt", a type of our turning from the world's system and following Christ. He "kept the passover," trusting in the blood of Christ for redemption from the curse of the Law. He then "passed through the Red Sea" when faced with annihilation from Pharaoh's army, experiencing the miracle of the parted waters when there was no other way of escape. This is a pattern set for all believers.

After we partake of Christ we may often be cornered with no way out except by His great power, which the Lord allows to teach us to trust in His ability to deliver us.

Moses never claimed to have great faith, but he continually demonstrated it. It was written of Moses that he "**... was very meek, above all the men which were upon the face of the earth" (Numbers 12:3 KJV).** Indeed, **"He gives His grace to the humble" (James 4:6 NASB).** The truly humble do not point to themselves, but to God, and Moses spent his life seeking to know Him and to reveal Him to His people. Many today have reduced faith to nothing more than having a faith in one's own faith, which is a diversion and the root of pride. True faith has God alone as its object, and Moses' life is a great example of such faith.

Joseph

The story of Joseph (Genesis 37-50) is one of the most marvelous in the entire Bible. Joseph also was a character type of the Christ who was to come and deliver His people. He was deceitfully sold into bondage through the jealousy of his older brothers, yet, the hand of God was upon him, not only to deliver him, but to make him a deliverer. Even in slavery, confidence in God can bring prosperity, as it was written of Joseph:

And his master saw that the Lord was with him, and that the Lord made all that he did to prosper in his hand.

And Joseph found grace in his sight, and he served him: and he made him overseer over his house,

and all that he *had he put into his hand* (Genesis 39:3-4).

Joseph's master, Potiphar, trusted Joseph's integrity so implicitly that he did not even bother to know the state of his own household. Although Potiphar's wife made continual attempts to seduce Joseph, he kept his integrity and rejected her advances. Joseph rejected her because he did not want to commit a sin against God. Faith in God can keep our way pure, even in the midst of the most difficult temptations.

Joseph's righteousness resulted in his being falsely accused, and unrighteously persecuted, eventually landing him in prison. Such unfairness and misunderstanding can be one of the most difficult tests of all. Many believe that because they serve the Lord that everything should always go well for them. However, the testimony of Scripture verifies that it is because of our righteousness that we suffer persecution and be mistreated. The Lord Jesus Himself, the most righteous man who will ever walk the earth, is our greatest example of this.

Regardless of the mistreatment, Joseph remained faithful. This led to his finding favor even while in prison, and continued the process of working such character in him that he could be exalted to one of the most powerful positions in the land. All of the trials that come our way are allowed for the same reason. We are called to an even higher position than Joseph attained at the right hand of Pharaoh—we are called to sit at the right hand of the throne of God! Like Joseph, this requires preparation. *Every* trial that comes our way is an opportunity to grow in faith. We must perceive them properly; as James said, they are more precious than gold.

The Psalmist used Joseph as an illustration of the Lord's faithfulness in carrying out His purposes through His people:

> **He sent a man before them, Joseph, who was sold as a slave. They afflicted his feet with fetters. He himself was laid in irons; until the time that His word came to pass, the Word of the Lord tested him. The king sent and released him, the ruler of peoples, and set him free. He made him lord over his house, and ruler over all his possessions (Psalms 105:17-21, NASB).**

The record of Joseph's journey from his homeland, to Egypt, to prison, and finally to the palace, spans only four chapters in the Bible, but it took thirteen years! He was seventeen years old when he was sold into bondage. When he finally stood before Pharaoh he was a man of thirty (see Genesis 41:46).

Joseph's faith had been severely tested and tried. All along the way he had been falsely accused and mistreated. Yet, he did not give up, nor did he walk away from his fellowship with God. The Lord had His hand on Joseph the whole time, preparing him to be a deliverer for his people and a forerunner in the building of a nation called Israel.

The people who walk in victory are the ones who will not give up. Their confidence is in God alone, and they refuse to live burdened under the circumstances. They maintain their walk with God—worshipping, praying and reading the Scriptures. They keep their confidence that Jesus Christ means what He says and that He will lead them daily to overwhelming victory.

David

Many books have been written on the trials and triumphs of David. When he was chosen by God to be Israel's second king he was just a shepherd boy, a young member of a most humble profession, and he came from the small, insignificant town of Bethlehem. In that time, the place of one's residence reflected his social rank. Even David's own family did not give him notice, but God was pleased to raise him from his low estate and place him upon the throne. The Lord delights in confounding the wise and strong of this world by raising up the lowly and the weak. It is not our rank with men that matters, but rather our rank with God.

God's dealings with David in preparing him for the palace is another one of the most interesting and inspiring stories of the Bible. David's victory over the giant Goliath instantly raised him to the status of one of the great warriors of his people, yet he had no training as a soldier and was too young to enter the army. With a small sling, but with huge faith, he faced the giant and prevailed. This has been a witness to every succeeding generation that whatever we have, combined with true faith in God, will be enough.

David went on to become a mighty man of war with the weapons of his day, but he never forgot the one Who empowered him. Although David was one of the greatest warriors of his day, it was not his ability to wage war that made him "a man after God's own heart." He earned that title because he was a *worshipper*. True worship is not for wimps—it is for the great of heart, those whose faith in God is greater than their fear of enemies—even giant enemies.

David's psalms of praise and worship reveal a deep love for God, thankfulness for His salvation, as well as a readiness to admit his own sins. David could never be accused of being lukewarm. He would do great exploits for the Lord, and then have some great failures. The "man after God's own heart," also fell into adultery and murder in one of the most grievous and deceptive incidences recorded in the Scripture. However, even though he was then the king, he had not forgotten how to humble himself, and God gives His grace to the humble.

Another illuminating account of David's response to serious trouble is found in I Samuel 30. Before he became king and while he was still fleeing from Saul, David, his six hundred men and their families, had set up camp in the city of Ziklag. The men left town to do battle, but when they returned the city had been burned and all the women, children and possessions had been taken as spoil by the Amalekites.

David's own men were so grieved that they talked of stoning him, considering that it was all David's fault. This was turning into a bad day! David had lost everything too, and now his own men were turning on him. It is understandable that **"David was greatly distressed..."** But David had been in distress before and he knew the way out: **"...But David encouraged himself in the Lord" (I Samuel 30:6).**

How did he do this? He began to recall what God had said to him and all that God had done for him. Consider this psalm that David wrote:

I will bless the Lord at all times: his praise shall continually be in my mouth.

My soul shall make her boast in the Lord: the humble shall hear thereof, and be glad.

O magnify the Lord with me, and let us exalt his name together.

I sought the Lord, and he heard me, and delivered me from all my fears.

They looked unto him, and were lightened: and their faces were not ashamed.

The poor man cried, and the Lord heard him, and saved him out of all his troubles.

The angel of the Lord encampeth round about them that fear him, and delivereth them.

O taste and see that the Lord is good: blessed is the man that trusteth in him (Psalm 34).

David then sought God as to whether or not he should attempt to recover the loss. He did not assume any action, even with the pressure that was coming from his own men, until he had inquired of the Lord. Such faith will always receive a reply, and the Lord's response was specific: "... **Pursue: for thou shalt surely overtake them, and without fail recover all**" (I Samuel 30:8).

David rallied his men and went after the thieves. He not only recovered their families and their belongings, but they took so much spoil that gifts were sent to the elders throughout Judah. In this seemingly impossible situation, David did not succumb to discouragement or self-pity. Instead, he turned to God. True faith, even in the most pressing circumstances, will not turn us inward, but upward.

During this time of great trial in David's life it seemed as though everything had gone wrong. The great prophet, Samuel, had promised that he would become the next king, but instead the whole house of Israel was pursuing him, and he was living in caves and holes in the ground. At that point he had faced one of the most difficult tests possible for any man—the kidnapping of his loved ones, not to mention all of his possessions, as well as those of all of his faithful men. Even though it looked like everything in his life was going wrong, David still knew how to turn to the Lord. Even after his great moral failure, David knew how to turn to the Lord for help. This endeared him to the Lord to such a degree that it would even be said of the Son of God that He would sit upon "the throne of David." David established a seat of authority that would endure for all generations, because his confidence was in God.

The End of the Race

When the Bible speaks of running **"with patience the race set before us" (Hebrews 12:1)**, it is not speaking about a one hundred yard dash, but a race that will require endurance. Such endurance was exemplified by these patriarchs of the faith—Enoch, Noah, Abraham, Sarah, Moses, Joseph, David and many others. They all teach us that, regardless of how long it takes, and how many times we slip or fall, we must get up and keep going. True faith never quits.

Chapter Six

Confidence in Crisis

It should be no surprise to any child of God that Satan sets his heart on the most effective servants of the Lord. The more effective we are, the more buffeted our lives will be. This is permitted for an important reason—our growth! We can see this clearly in the life of Job, under the Old Covenant, and with Paul, under the New Covenant.

In Job's case, God actually asked Satan: **"Have you considered my servant Job?" (Job 1:8 NASB).** In the New Testament, the apostle Paul was continually beset by persecutions and afflictions, even storms and attacks from wild beasts. The attacks upon us can be physical in nature such as sickness or accidents, or even "natural," such as tornadoes, hurricanes, floods, droughts, etc.

The enemy can also use individuals or groups as agents of persecution. During any of these onslaughts, the pressure can be extreme and can seem almost unbearable. I say "almost" because the Lord has promised He would not permit any trial to come upon us which we are unable to bear, but He will make a way for us to escape (see I Corinthians 10:13). We must always keep this in mind. It is impossible for Satan to get a shot in when God is not looking. Regardless of what the trial is, the Scriptures are clear—nothing happens to us that God does not allow for our own good.

When all hell breaks loose on those considered to be God's favorites, the Lord usually does not immediately rush to their rescue. The theme of the book of Job is not: "Why do Christians suffer?" but "Will a man serve God for nothing? Will he continue to serve the Lord when immersed in suffering? Will he serve God when his friends forsake him? Will a man serve God when God is silent?"

In the book of Job, it appears that the Lord wanted to prove to Satan that His special servants do not follow Him just for the benefits He provides, but because He is Lord and He is worthy. When the Lord described Job's faithfulness, Satan accused Job of serving God because of the protection and wealth he had received.

> **So Satan answered the Lord and said, Does Job fear God for nothing? Have You not put a hedge around him, around his household, and around all that he has on every side? You have blessed the work of his hands, and his possessions have increased in the land.**

> **But now, stretch out Your hand and touch all that he has, and he will surely curse You to Your face, (Job 1:9-11).**

Notice the Lord did not deny His protection and blessing over Job's life. Satan had spoken truth. God had hedged Job around to protect him from evil forces that were set to destroy him. When the hedge was removed, Job's wealth was taken from him. The Lord allowed Job's suffering to prove his faithfulness. But what a blow Job suffered! Everything material for which Job had labored for years was suddenly taken away. Perhaps Job could have handled this loss easier if that had been all. But a father will give all he has for his family. The response from most survivors of natural disasters is: "Thank God, we still have one another. We will build again and start over." But Satan did not stop there. In the disaster that followed, Job's children were all killed.

Many believers have questioned why God would permit these family members to die. Some who have endured such tragedies have even quit serving the Lord, feeling that He could not care or else He surely would have not allowed such sorrow. Many times, others outside the family become judgmental and place the blame on the victims themselves, with voiced suspicions of hidden sin, often producing resentment and a root of bitterness. But Job withstood these tests and demonstrated that he served God because of love and trust—not because of His blessings or His hedge of protection. Understandably, the Lord was pleased with Job's handling of this incredible test and He told Satan:

> **Have you considered My servant Job, that there is none like him on the earth, a blameless and upright man, one who fears God and shuns evil? And still he holds fast to his integrity, although you incited Me against him, to destroy him without cause (Job 2:3).**

Satan's nature is the complete opposite of God's. His goal is to destroy whereas God's is to create. The history of the world will be a testimony for all eternity of the contrasts between these natures. True to his character, Satan persisted in his accusations against Job, telling God: "Let me strike his flesh and he will curse You."

Trusting His servant to withstand this new test, God granted permission for the devil to do anything but kill Job. The Lord's servant was soon covered with painful sores from head to foot. The pain was so excruciating, that Job sat on a garbage pile and scraped his sores with a piece of pottery. His wife felt Job would be better off dead. "Curse God and die," she said. Her perception of God was so warped, that she felt that the Lord would strike anyone dead who cursed Him. But again Job passed the test. He refused to murmur against the Lord.

Finally, the Lord allows us to see Job at his worst. When his religious friends showed up and sat in silence for seven days without giving a word of comfort, Job lost his composure. No doubt their judgmental attitudes came through before they even spoke. By now, Job was angry. In Job 3:1, he opened his mouth and for the next 35 chapters he bemoaned his bitterness toward God, his friends, and his life in general. The following are some of the discouragements that flooded his soul, and may likewise rise up in any of us under such pressure:

Let the day perish on which I was born...Why did I not die at birth?...I long for death; but there is none...would that God were willing to crush me, that He would loose His hands and cut me off...I will complain in the bitterness of my soul...You

(God) did frighten me with dreams...Have I sinned? What have I done?...He (God) will not allow me to get my breath, but saturates me with bitterness...I loath my own life...I will give full vent to my complaint; I will speak in the bitterness of my soul...God, I wish You would just leave me alone; let me be neutral...The just and blameless man is a joke...I desire to argue with God...(To his friends) sorry comforters are you all....

God was listening but did not rebuke Job for his strong words until he made a serious mistake—he began to justify himself with comments similar to the following:

I don't have a problem with lust...I don't lie...I am not deceitful...I walk righteously...I am not tempted by women...I treat my employees right...I help the poor...I do not love money...I am not proud like some men are...I paid for everything I ever used or ate.

Doesn't that sound like the self-righteous Pharisee Jesus described in Luke 18? If any person wants to stir up the Lord's anger, let him begin to claim his own goodness. Thus, God began speaking in no uncertain terms to reveal His displeasure with Job's claims:

Who do you think you are, Job? Where were you when I made the worlds? When did you get so smart that you could figure out righteousness? Where did you get so much wisdom?

True to his character and sensitivity to the Lord, in spite of all of his suffering, Job quickly repented, falling on his face and crying: **"I have heard of you by the hearing of the ear, but now my eye sees You. Therefore I abhor myself, and repent in dust and ashes"** (Job 42:5-6).

After Job's repentance, the Lord required him to pray for his friends who had persecuted him. Then the Lord healed him, restored his wealth and gave him ten more children— seven sons and three daughters. Through this we see a five step path to victory in the midst of trials:

(1) Endure with patience.
(2) Look for a greater revelation of the Lord in the midst of the trials.
(3) Acknowledge and repent of whatever self-justification or self-righteousness may surface in our hearts.
(4) Pray for our persecutors and those who may have misjudged us.
(5) Acknowledge that the ways of God are greater than our ways, and they can always be trusted.

Even though Job's life conveys many personal weaknesses, God calls him a man of patience in the New Testament:

Indeed we count them blessed who endure. You have heard of the perseverance of Job and seen the end intended by the Lord—that the Lord is very compassionate and merciful (James 5:11).

Seldom do we ever pass one of God's tests with a perfect score. He is often far more pleased with us than we are with ourselves. While Job did not pass these tests without some mistakes, his patience was remarkable. Job suffered the loss of his wealth and children without a word of protest or any evidence of discouragement. Even when he lost his health, he remained true and positive and did not complain until his wife and friends misjudged him.

Surely it is satisfying to know of the Lord's forgiveness for those of us who have spoken in haste, anger and pain. After Job confessed and asked for forgiveness, it was as though he had never complained; he was called an example of patience and endurance.

It should be noted that Job did not have the benefit of most of the Old Testament revelation about Satan—and none of the New Testament's understanding. He was not aware that the devil was the cause of his troubles. The general theology of his time was that everything both good and evil came from God, which is probably why his wife told him to just curse God and die. This remains the shallow understanding of many today.

However, in the New Testament the revelation of our adversary is made clear. We do want to submit to God, and to the trials that He allows in our lives, but that does not include submitting to Satan and his attempts to destroy us. Believers are taught how to resist the devil, and how to recognize some of his devices and schemes. Jesus said: **"The thief (devil) comes only to steal, and kill, and destroy; I came that they might have life, and might have it abundantly" (John 10:10 NASB).**

The same devil who attacked Job also set out to hinder and torment the apostle Paul. In II Corinthians 12:7, Paul tells of a time when he cried out to God for relief from **"a thorn in the flesh."** He had previously testified of many perils, hardships and beatings but apparently this "thorn" was too much for the apostle. We do not know precisely what this thorn was, although Paul calls it **"a messenger of Satan to buffet me" (II Corinthians 12:7b, NASB).** Whatever the thorn was, it was a severe test for Paul.

The Scriptures tell us he prayed three times for the Lord to remove this thorn before he received any kind of answer. I agree with Jack Taylor, who said he did not believe Paul prayed three little short prayers but that he had three long sessions of crying out to God over this problem. He earnestly sought God in prayer and intercession. Without question, Paul knew how to pray and get answers. Yet, in this most difficult problem, the Lord would not give him any relief. Paul kept praying until he heard from God. When the Lord answered: **"My grace is sufficient for you, for My strength is made perfect in weakness" (II Corinthians 12:9a)**, Paul then submitted to the trial without complaint.

In essence, the Lord was saying: "You have all you need in me. To make you trust even more upon My grace, so that I can trust you with even greater revelation, the thorn will remain to keep you humble and dependent on Me. If I do not allow the devil to buffet you, you will get puffed up with all the supernatural revelations and miracles you have received."

Rev. Jack Taylor said, as far as he could determine, every problem any Christian could ever face is listed in Paul's response to God's answer to him in 2 Corinthians 12:10:[1]

Therefore I will boast all the more gladly about my weaknesses, so that Christ's power may rest upon me. That is why, for Christ's sake, I delight in weaknesses, in insults, in distresses, in persecutions, in necessities. For when I am weak, then I am strong.

Let us examine each one of these problems:

(1) **Weaknesses.** It may sound strange, but the devil often will not attack your weak areas because you tend to guard these dimensions of your life. Rather, Satan will often hit you where you feel the strongest. It is in those areas where we sometimes feel pride, which opens the door to God's resistance and gives the devil access.

God said "…for My strength is made perfect in weakness." That statement may be difficult for us to understand and accept. We are educated (wrongly) to believe that we must be strong to overcome and to earn God's approval. Yet, Ephesians 6:10 tells us to **"be strong *in the Lord* and in the power of *His might*"** with the emphasis on *"in the Lord."*

God has placed a hedge about you, and Satan can harm you only with God's permission. If God permits an attack upon your life, all the strength you can muster will not prevail against the enemy. Any sort of pride in our own strength will simply provide an open door to Satan.

The weakness of man's strength is illustrated in Uzziah who had a reputation almost equal to Solomon's. He began to reign in Judah when he was only 16 and reigned for 52 years. During this time he conquered the nations surrounding Israel and Judah, and made them pay tribute:

And he made devices in Jerusalem, invented by skillful men, to be on the towers and the corners, to shoot arrows and large stones. So his fame spread far and wide, for he was marvelously helped till he became strong.

But when he was strong his heart was lifted up, to his destruction, for he transgressed against the Lord his god by entering the temple of the Lord to burn incense on the altar of incense.

So Azariah the priest went in after him, and with him were eighty priests of the Lord—valiant men.

And they withstood King Uzziah, and said to him, It is not for you, Uzziah, to burn incense to the lord, but for the priests, the son of Aaron, who are consecrated to burn incense. Get out of the sanctuary, for you have trespassed! You shall have no honor from the Lord God.

Then Uzziah became furious; and he had a censer in his hand to burn incense. And while he was angry with the priests, a leprosy broke out on his forehead, before the priests in the house of the Lord, beside the incense altar.

And Azariah the chief priest and all the priests looked at him, and there, on his forehead, he was leprous; so they thrust him out of that place. Indeed he also hurried to get out, because the Lord had struck him.

King Uzziah was a leper until the day of his death. He dwelt in an isolated house, because he was a leper; for he was cut off from the house of the Lord. Then Jotham his son was over the king's house, judging the people of the land, (II Chronicles 26:15-21).

Thus, it was not weakness which caused this man of God to fall—it was his strengths that led to pride. When Uzziah felt weak and in need of God, he was used in a marvelous way to lead and govern the nation of Israel. God's power is truly made perfect in our weaknesses.

(2) **Insults.** Job and Paul both suffered insults from their detractors. David, as king, was even cursed by Shemei when he was retreating from Jerusalem to escape from his own son. Shemei who had waited for such an opportunity to express his hostility, shouted curses at David and threw stones from the hillsides. Abishai, one of the bravest of David's mighty men, asked permission from the king to take off Shemei's head with a sword. David's response to this request shows remarkable humility and wisdom:

And David said to Abishai and all his servants, "See how my son who came from my own body seeks my life. How much more now may this Benjamite? Let him alone, and let him curse; for so the Lord has ordered him.

It may be that the Lord will look on my affliction, and that the Lord will repay me with good for his cursing this day" (II Samuel 16:11-12 NKJV).

Have you considered that the persecution and afflictions that come against us from men can actually lead to God's grace being extended toward us? Paul's words, recorded in II Corinthians, were basically an echo of David's cry. *I will glory in all this slander and cursing so that the power of Christ will rest upon me.*

(3) **Distresses.** When it looked as if there was no way out of a dilemma, Paul knew the Lord would make a way. Thus, he learned to be content in whatever circumstance he found himself (Philippians 4:11).

Once when travelling as a prisoner to Rome, Paul's ship found itself in grave trouble. When all of his shipmates lost hope during a vicious storm (Acts 27), Paul kept his confidence, praying for fourteen days until God spoke. The ship would be lost but Paul and all 276 on board would be saved. Though there was no visible evidence for days, Paul cheered everyone with words of hope. **"I believe God..."** he said (Acts 27:25).

(4) **Persecutions.** No man of God ever suffered more for preaching the gospel than Paul. Some Bible scholars believe the background for II Corinthians 12 was Paul's stoning outside the city of Lystra. At the point of death, he was caught up into the third heaven where he was given special revelations. His comrades in ministry thought he was dead. After all, as Jack Taylor said, "He wasn't stoned with pea gravel."

When Paul's spirit returned to his body, he slowly crawled out of the pile of stones and probably said, "Let's go back to town, fellows, and witness for the Lord." They went back into the city, testifying to the same people who had stoned him and left him for dead. No wonder these early Christians "turned the world upside down." Satan cannot stop a person with so much confidence in God that he receives persecutions with thankfulness.

During the Nazi occupation of Holland, Corrie Ten Boom lived with her sister and father in Haarlem, Netherlands, a small city near Amsterdam. The family provided a hiding place in their home for Jews who were being sought by the

Nazis. Betrayed by someone in the city, the Ten Booms were arrested and sent to concentration camps. Corrie's father died in a distant prison, and her sister slowly withered until she died while residing in the same camp with Corrie. Corrie survived the concentration camp and went on to become a powerful witness for the Lord.

Before her death at age 89, Corrie had traveled the world speaking for the Lord, emphasizing how Christians should be prepared to endure persecution rather than expect to be rap-tured (caught up) before great tribulation. She warned that teaching an "escape mentality" is speculative and not based on Bible doctrine or her personal observations. She said:

> I have been in countries where the saints are already suffering terrible persecution. In China the Christians were told: "Don't worry. Before the tribulation comes, you'll be raptured." Then came a terrible persecution. Many Christians were tortured to death. Later I heard a bishop from China say sadly: "We failed. We should have made the Christians strong for persecution, rather than telling them Jesus would come and take them away."

> Turning to me he said: 'You still have time to tell the people how to prepare for persecution, how to stand when tribulation comes, to stand and not faint.

> I feel I have a divine mandate to go and tell the people of the world that it's possible to be strong in the Lord Jesus in tribulation. Since I have already gone to prison for Jesus' sake, and since I met that bishop from China, I find Scripture I think I can use in times of tribulation. Then I write it down and learn it by heart. There would be differences of opinion as to whether we will go

through the great tribulation, but for sure God$_2$ has promised to shake everything that can be shaken.^{2}

Corrie Ten Boom's words may seem a bit unusual to Christians in America, but why should the Lord make us exceptions when it concerns sacrificing our lives for the Name of Jesus Christ?

We should not be dogmatic regarding eschatological teachings concerning a pre-tribulation or post-tribulation rapture of the church. However, I feel it would be much healthier to prepare for tribulation and suddenly be caught up before great tribulation than to expect an escape only to be compelled to face what the Chinese Christians were surprisingly forced to face—denial of Christ as Lord or torture and death. Regardless of whether the rapture will come before or after *the* tribulation, tribulation can come upon the church at any time and in any place, and we should endeavor to be prepared at all times to endure it with grace and courage.

(5) **Necessities.** Necessities refer to that which we must do that we probably wish we didn't have to do. We may disdain the word "duty" but most of the work in the home and the church are done by those who simply see what needs to be done and do it. The apostle Paul takes note of this attitude in I Corinthians 9:16: **"For if I preach the gospel, I have nothing to boast of, for necessity is laid upon me; yes, woe is me if I do not preach the gospel!"**

There are times when a pastor may not feel like preaching on Sunday morning—yet the calling remains, and he just does his best. The same is true with fathers and mothers, school teachers and students, employers and employees, and others.

The work must be done, so they do it, "not being weary in well doing."

Finally, Paul also gloried in "unanswered prayer" or a "no answer." In Paul's situation, he did hear from God but the answer was "no". Have you ever felt that things would be all right in your life if God would simply say *something* to you, even if it is "no"?

Just as Job and Paul finally heard from God, so will you if you maintain your confidence and your persistence. Neither Job nor Paul heard what they actually wanted to hear. Paul thought God would say: "All right, Paul. You've done your best so I'll take this buffeting away from you. I'll let you out from under this pressure." But God didn't say that. Instead He said, "I'm not giving you what you asked for because you already have all that you need. All that really matters is you have My favor."

Of course, God's favor doesn't always mean that circumstances will change. In Job's case, everything changed for the better, but this was not true with Paul. Outwardly, nothing changed for the better. But Paul obtained the victory in his heart. In writing to the Romans, Paul asked:

Who shall separate us from the love of Christ? Shall tribulation, or distress, or persecution, or famine, or nakedness, or peril, or sword? Just as it is written: For Thy sake we are being put to death all day long; We are considered as sheep to be slaughtered.

But in all these things we overwhelmingly conquer through Him who loved us (Romans 8:35-37 NASB).

Job's circumstances changed for the better when God answered his prayers. But circumstances do not have to change for us to be victorious. Things did not improve for Paul. It *may be* best for us to go through troubles than to go around them or pray ourselves out of their way. Truly, then the Lord can declare: "They serve Me because they love Me and not because of what they get from Me."

Whatever your convictions regarding the purposes of suffering, all of us are taught to believe that we can be confident in the Lord when we face crises. And as long as we are in this world and are determined to follow Jesus our Lord, we shall face tribulations. Before Jesus left to go to Heaven, He encouraged His disciples with these words: **"In the world ye shall have tribulation: but be of good cheer; I have overcome the world" (John 16:33).**

Chapter Seven

True Confidence and Divine Rest

There remains therefore a Sabbath rest for the people of God (Hebrews 4:9, NASB).

In Scripture, rest is equated with the Promised Land (see Hebrews 3-4). God has purposed to lead His family into a rest—not a rest *from* work, but a rest *in* work. When we come to fully abide in Him, regardless of what we have been called to do, it will not only be achievable, but we will find rest and refreshment as we do it.

The temptation in Eden was one of self-sufficiency. By knowing good and evil himself, man was told he would not need God. He could live independent from the Lord and make his own decisions about what was good or evil for his own life. So independence is both the cause and a result of the curse. Jesus limits entrance into His kingdom to those who have childlike (not childish) faith to accept whatever He has said. Notice the promise of Matthew 11:28-30 (NASB):

Come to Me, all who are weary and heavy-laden, and I will give you rest. Take My yoke upon you, and learn from Me, for I am gentle and humble in heart; and you shall find rest for your souls. For My yoke is easy, and My load is light.

Before giving these words, Jesus had already said that God could not reveal Himself to the wise and prudent—but only unto babes. Possibly the most significant characteristic of a baby is that he is completely dependent on his parents. This is in contrast to the independence that was at the root of the original temptation, which caused the separation between God and men. This also led to the curse upon the ground so that man could only reap by "the sweat of his brow," or by striving. When we take the yoke of Jesus, and depend upon Him, we find rest from the curse of striving. The apostle John wrote these words in his first epistle:

What we have seen and heard we proclaim to you also, that you also may have fellowship with us; and indeed our fellowship is with the Father, and with His Son Jesus Christ.

And these things we write, so that your joy may be complete (I John 1:3-4 NASB).

Fellowship literally means "two fellows in the same ship." That is the same as being yoked with Jesus. From the fall of Adam, God has been seeking fellowship with the creature He made in His own image. His first words after the fall were;

"Adam, where are you?" The complete plan of the tabernacle, as shown in the book of Exodus, was to fulfill God's desire to "dwell with man." The entire redemption purpose is to "bring many sons unto glory" to satisfy the Father heart of God.

Contentment

Paul wrote to the Philippians: **"I have learned, in whatsoever state I am, therewith to be content" (Philippians 4:11).** The Amplified Bible translates this verse:

> **... I have learned how to be content [satisfied to the point where I am not disturbed or disquieted] in whatever state I am...I have learned in any and all circumstances, the secret of facing every situation.**

According to *Vine's Dictionary of New Testament Words*, the definition of content is "to be sufficient, to be strong, to be enough for a thing or to be satisfied."

Most of the time when we think about contentment we think about a feeling— perhaps a feeling of satisfaction. Yet, Paul was speaking of more than just a feeling. God's definition of contentment could be interpreted as reigning over every circumstance, because we abide in Him who is over all. When we do this we have control over our own feelings or emotions and do not allow them to rule over us.

In that context, Paul says, "I have learned in whatsoever state I am, to reign over the circumstance." Paul wrote that from a prison cell! God's principal ideal for His people is that they will enter into a place where they will allow Him to be in control of every situation, thereby actively entering into His eternal Sabbath.

Jesus—Our Apostle of Rest

So then, brethren, consecrated and set apart for God, who share in the heavenly calling, thoughtfully and attentively consider Jesus, the Apostle and High Priest Whom we confessed as ours [when we embraced the Christian faith].

[See how] faithful He was to Him Who appointed Him [Apostle and High Priest], as Moses was also faithful in the whole household [of God] (Hebrews 3:1,2 Amplified).

Each leader, as an apostle (someone sent by God on a special mission), was designated by the Lord to lead His people into a place of rest. Throughout chapters 3 and 4 of Hebrews, the Scripture continually speaks about entering into rest, explaining why Israel missed out on this. The Church has sung for generations about crossing the Jordan and entering Canaan. Yet, most people mistakenly identify crossing the Jordan with entering Heaven.

Crossing Jordan was never meant to be a sign of crossing into heaven. Canaan certainly was not heaven for the Israelites. It signifies crossing over into battle, even though He had assured them of the victory and dominion. Our Promised Land is that place where God no longer has to treat us as babies, hand-feeding us as it were, but treats us as His sons and daughters who have entered into responsibility to reign with Him over all our enemies. Even so, it is to be a place of rest! It involves our entering the land of sowing and reaping, knowing that God has allowed us to be His co-laborers in the process.

Thus, when God selected Moses to lead His people into Canaan, it was to lead them into what He called "rest". This is not a state of "no work," but of working with Him instead of against Him. This is to enter into a heavenly calling, to a complete trust that our lives and destinies are under God's control, and that we can reign with Him. According to Scripture, we are all partakers of this heavenly calling: **"Therefore, as the Holy Spirit says,** *Today***, if you will hear His voice" (Hebrews 3:7 Amplified).**

This word *"Today"* appears five different times in chapters 3 and 4 of Hebrews. This message is not for tomorrow. This is not for the "hereafter." A Christian doesn't have to wait until death to have this victory. God is speaking about reigning over circumstances *today*.

Today, you can reign. *Today*, you can enter into rest. *Today*, you can have victory. *Today*, you can learn to have peace in your situation. As Paul did, we can learn, in the face of all kinds of difficult situations and circumstances to declare, "Hallelujah to God! He is my strength, and He will see me through. I don't have to be upset in this predicament. It will be exciting to walk with the Lord through these troubles."

Hear the Voice of God

Hearing God's voice is absolutely vital in these times. This is the quality that distinguished the patriarchs of our faith. They heard the voice of God and obeyed Him.

Without question, we must learn to be sensitive to what God is saying to us. Otherwise, when we confront these seemingly insurmountable problems we will not be abiding in His rest. We will be void of His peace.

Hebrews 3:19 notes the very reasons God's people failed to receive His provision: **"So we see that they were not able to enter [into His rest] because of their unwillingness to adhere to and trust and rely on God—unbelief had shut them out"** (Amplified).

These were God's people. They were following a divine plan. His blessings had been promised. Yet, they failed to receive. Unbelief had destroyed their ability to hear and obey God in the midst of the problems and circumstances.

Therefore, while the promise of entering His rest still holds and is offered [today], let us be afraid [to distrust it], lest any of you should think he has come too late and has come short of [reaching] it.

... So then, there is still awaiting a full and complete Sabbath rest reserved for the [true] people of God;

For he who has once entered into [God's] rest also has ceased from [the weariness and pain] of human labors, just as God rested from those labors peculiarly His own.

Let us therefore be zealous and exert ourselves and strive diligently to enter into that rest [of God]—to know and experience it for ourselves— that no one may fall or perish by the same kind of

unbelief and disobedience [into which those in the wilderness fell] (Hebrews 4:1,9-11 Amplified).

Coming out of Egypt

When the children of Israel came out of Egypt, their expectations were high. Following the great miracle at the Red Sea, they sang and danced in victory. "The horse and rider had been thrown into the sea," they shouted. Yet, a few days later they were murmuring and complaining.

For three days, they had walked beyond the Red Sea, and they were without water. Where was their God of miracles now? Instead of murmuring and complaining, they should have believed and said: "We don't know what God has in mind, but He will provide. The water will be made available. We will serve Him and walk with God no matter what."

All through the wilderness, God miraculously manifested Himself to Israel, yet, the miracles did not cause them to enter into rest. They saw the miracles, and they witnessed His provision for their every need. They had a pillar of fire by night and a cloud to follow by day, but they still failed to enter God's rest.

Miracles will occur for us along the way. But miracles are not God's normal way to lead us through life. Deuteronomy 8:2-3 tells us how God sought to prepare Israel for her time in Canaan:

And you shall (earnestly) remember all the way which the Lord your God led you these forty years in the wilderness, to humble you, and to prove you,

to know what was in your [mind and] heart, whether you would keep His commandments or not.

And He humbled you and allowed you to hunger, and fed you with manna, which you did not know, nor did your fathers know; that He might make you recognize and personally know that man does not live by bread only, but man lives by every word that proceeds out of the mouth of the Lord (Amplified).

God was attempting to prepare Israel for the giants that lived in Canaan. The children of Israel didn't know that fact. The Lord knew that, unless they were willing to subdue their flesh and take control over their emotions, they could never face the giants of Canaan. They were unprepared, and they never found their rest.

Why Israel Didn't Find God's Rest

I Corinthians 10 gives us some of the reasons why the Israelites did not enter the rest which God intended for them.

(1) **Lust.** **"Now these things are examples (warnings and admonitions) for us not to desire or crave or covet or lust after evil and carnal things as they did" (verse 6 Amplified).**

What were these people lusting after? According to Exodus 16, when the Israelites were without food, God gave them manna from heaven. Yet, they craved and lusted after that which God said they couldn't have at that time. In other words, they wanted to satisfy their taste buds with meats they had relished in Egypt rather than receive and enjoy the manna God was giving them from Heaven. Dissatisfaction, or discontentment, will always prevent us from entering God's rest.

Again, "entering His rest" is not the same as receiving His provisions. Like Israel, we can receive miracles and all manner of blessings and provisions from Him, yet still not enter His rest. James wrote about this:

> **What leads to strife (discord and feuds) and how do conflicts (quarrels and fightings) originate among you? Do they not arise from your sensual desires that are ever warring in your bodily members?**
>
> **You are jealous and covet [what others have] and your desires go unfulfilled; [so] you become murderers. [To hate is to murder as far as your hearts are concerned.] You burn with envy and anger and are not able to obtain [the gratification, the contentment and the happiness that you seek], so you fight and war. You do not have because you do not ask (James 4:1,2 Amplified).**

This passage reveals that a person cannot enter into rest as long as this kind of lust remains in his heart. It kept the children out of the promised land and continues to prevent many of God's people from living in the confidence of His divine rest.

(2) Idol worship. "Do not be worshippers of false gods as some of them were, as it is written, The people sat down to eat and drink [the sacrifices offered to the golden calf

**at Horeb] and rose to sport (to dance and give way to
jesting and hilarity)" (verse 7).**

Where do you suppose these Jews learned about worshipping a golden calf? The golden calf was a god of Egypt. Since they planned to return to Egypt (while Moses was on the mount receiving the Ten Commandments), they wanted to be accepted in Egypt, so they made an Egyptian god.

Egypt represents the old life, the one we lived before Jesus became our Lord. Once we become children of God, we need to destroy every god of Egypt. That frees us from the temptation of wanting to return to our old way of life. It frees us from building imaginary gods in our minds and fantasizing over former pleasures. We will never learn to enter our rest while yearning for the gods of our past.

(3) Fornication. "We must not gratify evil desire and indulge in immorality as some of them did—and twenty-three thousand [suddenly] fell dead in a single day!" (verse 8).

God does not make regulations just to put us under bondage and take away our joy and freedom. God has placed these admonitions in Scripture because He loves us and knows what will bring us into rest and what will keep us from it.

The Israelite men were tempted by the Moabite women who were beautiful to look upon. God had forbidden this relationship, but they ignored His warning. The tragic result was that they died in shame and their bones were bleached in the wilderness. Samson is another example of this truth. Even though he was a man who had the power of God upon his life, he died prematurely, and in bondage to the Philistines, because he failed to heed God's command in this area. Fornication will always lead to bondage and destruction.

(4) **Tempting God**. **"We should not tempt the Lord [try His patience, become a trial to Him, critically appraise Him and exploit His goodness] as some of them did—and were killed by poisonous serpents" (verse 9).** The Scripture here is speaking of the presumption of trying to pressure God into doing our bidding. This is the "jumping off the temple" syndrome. It is making God prove Himself. Just as Jesus rejected that attempted snare of the devil, so we must refuse in like manner.

(5) **Murmuring**. **"Nor discontentedly complain as some of them did and were put out of the way entirely by the destroyer [death]" (verse 10).**

If we are not guilty of any of the other four sins preventing divine rest, some of us can plead no contest to being murmurers and complainers. Note that I said some complained, not all. John Wesley said, "I would no more fret than I would curse."

The opposite of a complaining spirit is a thankful spirit. As the psalm states, we **"enter His gates with thanksgiving, and His courts with praise" (Psalm 100:2-4 NASB).** If we do not learn to sing and praise the Lord we will ultimately murmur and complain. In the process, we will not only be denied our rest, we may be given over to the destroyer. Praise is the language of faith, and without faith it is impossible to please God. Complaining is the language of doubt, and those who doubt do not receive from the Lord (James 1:6,7).

The Scripture plainly teaches that God has provided a place of rest—where we can completely and totally trust Him in every circumstance. This is available to every child of God. That clearly is the heart of I Corinthians 10:13 (Amplified):

> **For no temptation—no trial regarded as enticing to sin [no matter how it comes or where it leads]— has overtaken you and laid hold on you that is not common to man—that is, no temptation or trial has come to you that is beyond human resistance and that is not adjusted and adapted and belonging to human experience, and such as man can bear. But God is faithful [to His Word and to His compassionate nature], and He [can be trusted] not to let you be tempted and tried and assayed beyond your ability and strength of resistance and power to endure, but with the temptation He will [always] also provide the way out—the means of escape to a landing place that you may be capable and strong and powerful patiently to bear up under it.**

We are told that God was not pleased with the Israelites. When He is not pleased with us, there is no way we can enter into rest. Enoch is a great example of one who pleased God by walking in faith with the Almighty in the midst of a perverse generation. Our rejection of the normal unbelieving, ungodly behavior of this world and walking out our faith and confidence in the Lord thrills Him. There is no other way to enter into His rest.

Chapter Eight

Restoring Lost Confidence

The book of Hebrews was written by a man who recognized that something had been lost by the Jewish believers in Jerusalem since the glorious days following Pentecost. The first apostles were no longer around to keep the believers encouraged and ready to face persecution. The confidence of many in the Hebrew church was at a low ebb. The name of Jesus no longer burned in their hearts when they spoke of Him.

The Jewish believers had hoped, even expected, their kinsmen to readily accept Jesus as the Messiah. To their dismay many Jews rejected the new believers and clung to their old form of worship. These New Testament Hebrews were despised by their own countrymen. Times were rough. Where were the miracles of the early days? Some began to think that perhaps the Old Covenant was better than the New. The pressure to return to their former rituals and the seeming security of the Law was strong and some were succumbing to it.

Under the Holy Spirit's inspiration, the author of the book of Hebrews set out to reveal the glory of the person of Jesus Christ in order to restore the confidence of these believers. He also warned them of the path which their forefathers had taken in unbelief and disobedience which had kept them from entering God's rest:

> **See to it, brothers, that none of you has a sinful, unbelieving heart that turns away from the living God. But encourage one another daily... so that none of you may be hardened by sin's deceitfulness. Therefore... (Hebrews 3:12,13; 4:1 NIV).**

After "therefore", the author of Hebrews admonishes his brothers nine times with the words "let us". These are worthwhile admonitions for all believers to consider.

Let Us Fear (Hebrews 4:1)

It seems incongruous for the Lord to exhort us to fear in order to enter into His rest. Is not fear the opposite of faith? Are we not told 365 times in the Scriptures to "be not afraid"? Paul even says, **"God has not given us a spirit of fear" (II Timothy 1:7).** Without question there is an unholy fear based on unbelief and anxiety; but the Bible also speaks of a holy fear, a healthy fear. There is a godly fear that is mingled with love for Him, which is the foundation of a true faith in Him. The latter fear causes a reverence for God and His Word, and provides a caution against disobedience. It is this kind of fear that is addressed in one of the greatest hymns of the church, *Amazing Grace*, "It was grace that taught my heart to fear and grace my fears relieved."

The pure and holy fear of the Lord is simply the acknowledgement of reality. It is knowing the truth of who God really is, and who we are in relation to Him. It is the reverential fear of the Lord that motivated us to bow before Him and be saved. It was the same kind of fear which motivated Noah to obey God and build an ark. It was this holy fear that came upon the early church when Ananias and Sapphira were slain by the Holy Spirit for lying to Him: **"And great fear came upon the whole church, and upon all who heard these things"** (Acts **5:11 NASB**).

It is this holy fear that Solomon described when he exhorted: **"By the fear of the Lord, men depart from evil"** (**Proverbs 16:6**). The Scriptures strongly imply that it is because men lack the fear of the Lord that they live in evil. Holy fear brings holy confidence and holy living. Unholy and unhealthy fear destroys confidence as is illustrated by Israel's fearing the giants of Canaan and disobeying the voice of the Lord: **"The fear of man bringeth a snare, but whoso putteth his trust in the Lord shall be [set on high] safe"** (**Proverbs 29:25**).

When Paul told Timothy that God has not given us a spirit of fear, he used the Greek word *deilia*, which literally translated means "intimidation by man." To have a deep-seated fear of man is both unhealthy and ungodly.

However, it is beneficial to have a holy fear of the Lord. In speaking about the fear of God, we have diluted its meaning, declaring it to be a light recognition that God exists and we should reverence Him. Then we continue in our disobedience. The Israelites exemplify this attitude:

> **Therefore, let us fear lest, while a promise remains of entering His rest, any one of you should seem to have come short of it. For indeed we have had good news preached to us, just as they also; but the word they heard did not profit them, because it was not united by faith in those who heard (Hebrews 4:1-2 NASB).**

Because of their lack of this holy fear, the Israelites did not act on God's good news preached to them. Rather, **"they were overthrown in the wilderness" (I Corinthians 10:5b).** Of an estimated two million people who left Egypt, only two entered the Promised Land. That is "one in a million." The writer of Hebrews is exhorting Christians that this should remind them of the seriousness of losing this holy fear. How many of God's servants, who began their walks with the Lord with such promise just as Israel, have followed their example?

> **Now all these things happened unto them for examples [types]: and they are written for our admonition...Wherefore let him that thinketh he standeth take heed lest he fall (I Corinthians 10:11,12).**

Therefore, if we desire to keep or restore our confidence, let us choose the fear of God. A lack of holy fear causes sin, and sin causes unbelief, and unbelief results in a hardened heart. A hardened heart can put us in serious jeopardy of falling short of the grace of God.

Let Us Be Diligent (Hebrews 4:11)

God is sovereign, yet, He does not make puppets of people. He requires us to make choices in how we are to serve Him. And He is pleased to "reward them who diligently seek Him." Entering into rest does not mean simply relaxing with an attitude that whatever will be will be.

The nation of Israel illustrates that this lackadaisical approach to the promises of God will leave us wandering around in the wilderness. Complaining against God, and the leadership He provided through Moses, cost them their inheritance. The author of Hebrews warns against passivity: **"... we must pay much closer attention to what we have heard, lest we drift away from it" (Hebrews 2:1 NASB).**

I have observed that most backsliders do not just suddenly stop trusting and serving the Lord. They drift away little by little as their life loses its vibrancy for the things of the Lord. The same is true of churches and movements within the church. Almost every spiritual awakening in history likewise gradually lost its fervency, usually becoming trapped in a form of godliness and religious rituals rather than captured by the Lord Himself. Some of these movements have even tried to maintain a form of godliness by maintaining the dress and the lifestyle of the time period in which their movement was initiated.

All of us could name denominations or even independent churches which at one time flowed with the life of God, but are now dying or already dead. This will happen to us all if we do not maintain our diligence in always seeking to draw closer to the Lord.

The story in Matthew 15:21-28 illustrates how determination or diligence is a vital part of faith. Jesus withdrew from the crowds in Galilee and took His disciples on a retreat in the district of Tyre and Sidon. While Jesus was relaxing with His disciples in Gentile country, a Canaanite woman began to follow them, crying out in her desperation: **"Have mercy on me, O Lord, Son of David; my daughter is cruelly demon possessed" (verse 22 NASB).**

It is not mentioned where she learned the promises of the Old Testament, but she recognized Jesus as the Son of David, the promised Messiah birthed through the descendants of David. In her heart she knew Jesus could free her daughter. Yet when she cried out to Jesus, He **"did not answer her a word" (verse 23)**.

The Lord's silence did not silence her. She was determined to get help for her daughter. Finally, the disciples became annoyed with her constant shouting. **"Send her away,"** they said to Jesus, **"for she is shouting out after us" (verse 23).**

Jesus probably spoke the disciples' thoughts regarding the woman: **"I was sent only to the lost sheep of the house of Israel" (verse 24).** Or perhaps He spoke of His primary mission to go first to the Jews. But this woman obviously knew the teaching of the Old Testament that the Messiah would also be a light to the Gentiles. Therefore, she was not deterred in her pursuit to get help for her tormented daughter. Her overwhelming burden was clearly shown in her words: **"Lord, help me" (verse 25).** This is possibly the most simple but powerful prayer we can utter!

However, looking down at her weeping at His feet, Jesus made what appeared to be a heartless reply: **"It is not good to take the children's bread and throw it to dogs" (verse 26).** This statement accurately expressed the sentiments of the average Jew toward the Gentiles. Surely God would not take what belonged to Israel and give it to Gentile dogs. But Jesus, who never did anything that He did not see the Father doing, had already "seen" what He was going to do.

Most people are easily offended—especially by racial remarks. But this woman's determination was greater than her personal feelings, or concern for what others thought of her. She rose above this seeming slap in the face by the Son of God to respond with a profound humility: **"Yes, Lord,"** she said, **"but even the dogs feed on the crumbs which fall from their masters' table"** (verse 27).

Jesus was not being heartless; He was seeking to reveal her great heart to His own disciples. Later, when many of them would be sent to the Gentiles with the gospel, they would remember her. **"O woman, your faith is great,"** He exclaimed. **"Be it done for you as you wish"** (verse 28). Her daughter was healed instantly. Her faith was clearly revealed in her determination.

Many times the response of God to our needs and prayers will seem heartless to us, but we can count on the fact that God is never heartless. His response to His children will always be for their good, or the good of others who witness the faith, patience, and humility of His people when under pressure.

Faith is not passive. It is active. It is diligent. It fights and prevails. It is based on incontestable confidence in the Word of God which "violently takes the Kingdom of God by force" (see Matthew 11:12b). Let us therefore be determined to regain our confidence in God's promises and enter into the promise of divine rest with the same faith of the two great souls who made it from that first generation. Indeed, let us be diligent.

Let Us Hold Fast Our Confession
(Hebrews 4:14)

Four times in the book of Hebrews the author cautions believers to "hold fast". Each is worthy of noting here:

> **But Christ was faithful as a Son over His house whose house we are, if we hold fast (*kataschomen*) our confidence and the boast of our hope firm until the end (Hebrews 3:6 NASB).**

> **For we have become partakers of Christ, if we hold fast (*kataschomen*) the beginning of our assurance firm until the end (Hebrews 3:14 NASB).**

> **Since then we have a high priest who has passed through the heavens, Jesus the Son of God, let us hold fast (*kratomen*) our confession (Hebrews 4:14 NASB).**

> **Let us hold fast (*kataschomen*) the confession of our hope without wavering, for He who promised is faithful (Hebrews 10:23 NASB).**

The Greek word *kataschomen* literally means: "to hold in a firm grasp, to possess, to occupy." The word *kratomen* means: "to seize, grasp or adhere to." There is little difference in the two words except *kratomen* adds to seize or to be in the process of grasping our confession while *kataschomen* emphasizes occupying.

Many of God's people have a great beginning. Yet somewhere along their journey of faith, things begin to go wrong and suddenly they've lost a grip on their confidence. Israel had a great beginning in leaving the land of Egypt. God brought them out with a victory march through the Red Sea. What joy they experienced! But their initial faith to leave Egypt was not enough to enter Canaan. Moses told Israel why God had led them into the wilderness:

And you shall remember all the way which the Lord your God has led you in the wilderness these forty years, that He might humble you, testing you, to know what was in your heart, whether you would keep His commandments or not.

And He humbled you and let you be hungry, and fed you with manna which you did not know, nor did your fathers know, that He might make you understand that man does not live by bread alone, but man lives by everything that proceeds out of the mouth of the Lord (Deuteronomy 8:2,3 NASB).

We live by the word that *proceeds* from the mouth of the Lord, not the word that *proceeded*. It is good to remember the victories of the past, which can help give us confidence in future trials, but every new day requires fresh faith.

As we learn to "hold fast", there will be times when the winds of trial will blow hard against us. Satan constantly stands to oppose and accuse us. We overcome him as spoken in Revelation 12:11, **"because of the blood of the Lamb and because of the word of their testimony, and they did not love their life even to death" (NASB).** Let us briefly look at each of these foundations of the victorious life.

"The life of the flesh is in the blood" (Leviticus 17:11). That we have been given the blood of the Lamb means that we have been given His life. We can overcome just as He overcame because we actually have His life in us. What greater confidence could anyone have than the knowledge that Jesus Christ abides in him by His Holy Spirit? We may know this in our minds, but when that knowledge is transferred to our hearts so that we begin to live by that knowledge, the world will see it. Then Jesus will be the Word of our testimony, and like Him, we will freely lay down our lives. The most accurate definition of an "overcomer" may well be one who has fully laid down his own life and self-interests to give himself completely to God's purposes, to live by His life and to testify of His Word.

God spoke through Isaiah: **"I create the fruit of his lips" (Isaiah 57:17 Amplified).** Therefore, it is important that we speak words of faith rather than words of doubt. Jesus is the "high priest of our confession." Our confession must not simply be a formula we employ to get what we want. It is to be a lifestyle based on the Word of God which is alive and active in us.

The story of the Shunammite woman in II Kings 4 is a case in point. The prophet Elisha conducted meetings throughout the northern tribes of Israel. Shunam, in the territory of Issachar, was one of his favorite places to minister. A prominent woman of the area, who is left unnamed in the Scriptures, attended his meetings and regularly invited him and his servant, Gehazi, into her home for meals. She persuaded her husband that Elisha was a holy and deserving man of God and had him build an upper room in their house for Elisha and Gehazi.

One day while they were resting there, Elisha sent for the woman: **"Behold you have been very careful for us with all this care,"** he said to her, when she came to the room. **"What can I do for you? Would you be spoken for to the king or to the captain of the army?"** She answered: **"I live among my own people"** (II Kings 4:13 NASB). She was saying, in modern speech, "I am just a country lady and I am totally satisfied with my circumstances." Thus, she went about her duties feeling privileged to have the man of God in her home.

Elisha kept prodding Gehazi to come up with something he could do for the woman. Finally Gehazi mentioned he had noticed the woman had no son and her husband was an old man. Elisha excitedly sent for her again. "At this time next year," he said, "you shall have a son to love and raise." She could not believe his words. "Please," she begged, "Is this really true? You mean I am going to have a son of my own even though my husband is old...?" A son was born to her the next year. She nursed him until the child was weaned and then allowed him to follow his father in the fields. One day as he was playing in the fields, he was stricken with a dreadful headache and soon died in his mother's arms.

Then the woman remembered the word of the man of God: "You will have a son to raise." She calmly laid the boy on Elisha's bed and sent word to her husband that she had to leave to see the man of God. When he questioned her plans, she did not tell him of the boy's death, but quietly repeated her request to him. Though her husband was pictured as a gentle man who loved his wife, he probably was not a covenant believer. Her silence regarding the boy's death spoke two things: (1) she was convinced he would be raised from the dead, and (2) she did not want to risk hearing words of unbelief if she told her husband the reason for rushing to Elisha.

As Elisha was meditating in his house on Mount Carmel, he saw her in the spirit as she was speeding toward him. He sent Gehazi to determine why she was coming to him at such speed. Gehazi shouted to the woman: "Is it well with you? Is it well with your husband? Is it well with the child"? Amazingly she answered: "It is well!"

At Mount Carmel, she leaped from the buggy and grabbed the feet of Elisha. "Did I ask for a son from my Lord?" she said. "Did I not say, 'do not deceive me?' " Elisha felt the woman's burden and tried to console her by sending Gehazi to return to her house and lay his staff upon the child. But somehow she knew Gehazi lacked the Spirit's unction for the task. Finally, she persuaded Elisha to make the trip. On the way, they met Gehazi returning with the news the boy was not yet breathing.

Arriving at the upper room, Elisha entered alone and closed the door. Impressed to cover the boy with his body, he stretched out on him. Soon the child's body began to get warm. However, no life came. Elisha stood and walked back and forth in the room calling upon God for a flow of the Spirit on him. Once again, he stretched out upon the child. Then, life returned and the boy sneezed seven times.

We are not told how long Elisha stayed in the room before victory came. He simply prayed through—he did not quit until the boy was raised. Elisha called for the woman and handed the child to her—alive and well. She fell on the ground and worshipped the Lord. Standing fast on her confession: "It is well," God had given her son back to her. Let us hold fast to our confession, as she did.

Let Us Draw Near (Hebrews 4:16;10:22)

The idea of coming before the God of heaven with boldness was entirely new to the Jews. Their concept of the Lord had been established through the tabernacle. God hid Himself within the inner veil of the Most Holy Place. The High Priest appointed by the Lord was the only one allowed to enter His presence. The common priest could enter the Holy Place within the first tabernacle but not into the Most Holy Place where the presence of God was manifest in a cloud of brilliant light. Even the High Priest could not enter except once each year on the Day of Atonement. Before he entered, he had to go through a special sanctifying ritual so he could be declared cleansed from all sin.

The average Israelite could enter within the curtains surrounding the tabernacle where his sins were laid on the sacrifice at the altar of burnt offerings. A foreigner had to stay clear of the curtains. To suggest that a believer could enter God's presence with boldness was considered blasphemy by orthodox Jews, but this confidence we now have is exactly what makes the New Covenant better than the Old.

Our High Priest has entered into heaven to become our Mediator. He sits at the right hand of the throne of God. His blood has been sprinkled on the mercy seat once and for all. We have a Friend, an Elder Brother, who invites us to come boldly to the throne of grace because of His sprinkled blood. We have been justified by faith in His blood and have a right to enter the very presence of God.

The author of Hebrews provides us with helpful insight into the New Covenant believers' entrance to God's throne:

But you have come to Mount Zion and to the city of the living God, the heavenly Jerusalem, and to myriads of angels,

to the general assembly and church of the first-born who are enrolled in heaven, and to God, the Judge of all, and to the spirits of righteous men made perfect,

and to Jesus, the mediator of a new covenant, and to the sprinkled blood, which speaks better than the blood of Abel (Hebrews 12:22-24, NASB).

God is not Santa Claus, nor "the man upstairs", but neither is He untouchable. He is our Father and desires to fellowship with us. He delights to grant His mercy and favor to those who come through His Son, the Lord Jesus Christ.

As a youngster, I grew up on a farm in south Mississippi. A few miles from our home was a railroad line which climbed a steep incline known as "Teewunne Hill". During the depression years of the 1930s that hill was a key spot for hoboes to catch on or jump from the trains. Many of these men found their way to our home seeking food. They would most often come to the back door, knock, take off their battered hat, and ask for a handout. These timid men were anything but confident. They were road-worn, beaten, and defeated by life.

My mother was always kind and fed them to the full. On the farm, we did not have much money, but we had plenty to eat and were always willing to share with these hungry men. If they had known of my parents' grace, they would have come to the front door with confidence and boldness.

Many believers do not yet know of God's abundant grace and willingness to receive any who will come to Him. We stand at God's back door, as it were, with hat in hand, pleading our unworthiness rather than our position in Christ. We are not hoboes! We are sons of the Most High God and have a right to come to His front door, enter at His invitation, sit at His table, and say, "Pass the bread, please."

Let Us Press On to Maturity (Hebrews 5:11-14)

The prophet Hosea noted that God's people were destroyed for lack of knowledge, while the author of Hebrews addresses similar deficiencies in believers:

> **... you have become dull of hearing. For though by this time you ought to be teachers, you have need again for someone to teach you the elementary principles of the oracles of God, and you have come to need milk and not solid food.**
>
> **For everyone who partakes only of milk is not accustomed to the word of righteousness, for he is a babe.**
>
> **But solid food is for the mature, who because of practice have their senses trained to discern good and evil (Hebrews 5:11b-14 NASB).**

The teaching on Melchizedek is solid food for the spirit. A believer must know of the deep truths relating to our High

Priest in heaven if he or she is going to walk in confidence during times of trouble and persecution. But far too many Christians are satisfied with the most elementary level of God's revelation.

Who among us now really appreciates the Melchizedek type of the priesthood of Christ? Dull ears call for things which can be easily understood with little study or diligence. Some rest in their orthodoxy, their connection to the church and its fundamentals. All of this is important but it will not be enough to mature us, nor to bring us into confidence in the Lord.

This is not to be confused with simply having the mental capacity to understand. Spiritual truth must be spiritually discerned by spiritual minds. Such spiritual discernment is the result of the hunger to know God who is Spirit. After many years of following the Lord, Paul declared with deep feelings:

I count all things to be loss in view of the surpassing value of knowing Christ Jesus my Lord...that I may know Him, and the power of His resurrection (His priesthood ministry now) and the fellowship of His sufferings... (Philippians 3:8,10 NASB).

This will always be the primary quest of every true believer.

Trials Help Us to Mature

The Lord uses many ways to bring each believer to maturity. With this in mind He allows us to confront difficult problems. James and Paul both stated that trials were opportunities for spiritual growth which should be embraced with joy.

Consider it all joy, my brethren, when you encounter various trials,

knowing that the testing of your faith produces endurance.

And let endurance have its perfect result, that you may be perfect and complete, lacking in nothing (James 1:2-4 NASB).

...we also exult in our tribulations, knowing (in our spiritual knower) that tribulation brings about perseverance; and perseverance, proven character; and proven character, hope; and hope does not disappoint... (Romans 5:3-5 NASB).

God was using trials to bring His believers to maturity in Christ, but they often misinterpreted problems as an indication that God did not care for them, or was not keeping His promises. Many of these had come to Jesus as a result of problems, and obviously thought that by coming to Him all of their problems would be over. This same fallacy is believed by many today. Such usually fall away quickly. However, the true of heart and the spiritually mature will embrace problems in the light of their intended purpose. Problems are tests, and tests are meant to qualify us for promotion.

Responsibility

Sometimes the Lord gives us responsibilities that are beyond our strength or wisdom. This causes us to rise to a new level of relationship to Him. Deuteronomy 32:11-13 describes this process in an interesting metaphor:

Like an eagle that stirs up its nest,
That hovers over its young,
He spread His wings and caught them,
He carried them on His pinions.
The Lord alone guided him,
And there was no foreign god with him.
He made him ride on the high places of the earth...
(NASB).

Here God compares the training of His children to that of an eagle. The eagle builds its nest by placing a cushion of feathers on top of thorns. At the proper time the mother eagle stirs up the nest by pulling out the feathers and leaving a nest of thorns. The young bird becomes so uncomfortable that it is forced to climb on the mother eagle's back. The mother then glides out from the high nest, dipping to force the young eagle off of her back into the air by itself. If the young one does not learn quickly the mother will catch it before it crashes, but then she will just take it up to try again until it learns to fly alone.

Let Us Encourage One Another (Hebrews 10:24-25)

The most tender admonition of the author of Hebrews is written here:

Let us consider how to stimulate one another to love and good deeds, not forsaking our own assembling together, as is the habit of some, but encouraging one another; and all the more, as you see the day drawing near (NASB).

A paraphrase of these verses would be: "Let us be concerned for one another, keeping our minds busy thinking up ways to encourage one another to love and to be faithful. But we cannot do this if we stay away from the meetings as some have a habit of doing. This is more important now that we see the day of the Lord drawing near."

One major purpose for the local church meetings is to provide a place for us to encourage one another. To encourage means to "build courage." Courage is an area in which we should all be growing. We derive courage from knowing that we are all a part of a church family who will be there when we need them, who will understand our weaknesses and will help us to overcome them, who will love us in spite of the many mistakes that we all make. Solomon understood this need quite well, as he wrote:

> **Two are better than one...For if either of them falls, the one will lift up his companion. But woe to the one who falls when there is not another to lift him up...And if one can overpower him who is alone, two can resist him. A cord of three strands is not quickly torn apart (Ecclesiastes 4:9,10,12 NASB).**

One of the most important ministries that any Christian can have is that of an encourager. Joseph of Cyprus had such a ministry. He encouraged Christians of the early church in Jerusalem who had lost their property because of their testimony for Jesus. His name was changed from Joseph to "Barnabas" which means "Son of encouragement." It was no accident that Barnabas was so instrumental in bringing the great apostle Paul to the Gentiles, to the place where he could be released into that ministry.

After Paul's conversion the believers were not willing to associate with him because he had been such a persecutor of the church. But Barnabas, like most encouragers, always saw the best in people, and he responded very differently, as we read in Acts 9:26,27:

And when he (Paul) had come to Jerusalem, he was trying to associate with the disciples; and they were all afraid of him, not believing that he was a disciple.

But Barnabas took hold of him and brought him to the apostles and described to them how he had seen the Lord on the road, and that he had talked to him, and how at Damascus he had spoken out boldly in the name of Jesus (NASB).

Later Paul caused so much friction in Jerusalem that the church council sent him away to his home town of Tarsus. We might have never heard of Paul again if Barnabas had not sought him out and brought him to Antioch (see Acts 11:23-26). It was in Antioch that Paul and Barnabas received the call to become the first missionaries to the pagan world. It will always be the nature of the ministry of encouragement to help others to see and fulfill their destiny in Christ.

It is also noteworthy that Barnabas was also released into his own apostolic ministry with Paul. Whenever we help others we are also positioning ourselves to be helped by God. Those who devote themselves to helping others find their place in the body of Christ will not be left out, but will find themselves being promoted by God Himself.

When we begin to understand the significance of the ministry of encouragement, no one in the church will ever be without help in a time of discouragement. We should encourage others because they are our brothers and sisters, members of our own family, and they are the precious souls that our Savior gave His own life to save. Probably the greatest thing that anyone can do for a truly loving parent is to help his children, and this is one of the greatest things that we can do for God—we can love and encourage His children.

Let Us Lay Aside Encumbrances & Run the Race (Hebrews 12:1)

Therefore, since we have so great a cloud of witnesses surrounding us, let us also lay aside every encumbrance...and let us run with endurance the race that is set before us (Hebrews 12:1 NASB).

From Hebrews 12:1 emerge three significant truths — (1) The faith heroes and heroines listed in chapter 11 are now witnessing our race from the stands; (2) They disciplined themselves to lay aside every hindrance to their race for the Lord; (3) The race is not a one hundred yard dash but a race that will require endurance.

One of the most serious problems facing the church of our generation is that believers are losing heart and dropping out of the race. Fatigue sets in much faster when we try to carry the weight of secret sin, or cares of this life, with us. Others are disheartened with this world's hostility against the Christian faith, especially when it comes from family or friends who reject the Lord.

Our eyes are to rest upon Jesus Christ, our Lord:

...the author and perfecter of faith, who for the joy set before Him endured the cross, despising the shame, and has sat down at the right hand of the throne of God. For consider Him who has endured such hostility by sinners against Himself, so that you may not grow weary and lose heart (Hebrews 12:2,3 NASB).

To fix our eyes on Jesus is to continually be strengthened with His strength and His encouragement. Of all of the witnesses who may be looking down upon this last day ministry of the church, Jesus is the foremost, and He is the One that we can look up to see, for encouragement at any time.

The apostle Paul advises us concerning our earthly race:

(1) We have been given a ministry to fulfill: **"Therefore, since we have this ministry, as we received mercy, we do not lose heart" (II Corinthians 4:1 NASB).**

(2) If we give up, people who need us will be discouraged and tempted to quit also: **"For all things are for your sakes, that the grace which is spreading to more and more people may cause the giving of thanks to abound to the glory of God. Therefore we do not lose heart..." (II Corinthians 4:15,16a NASB).** We are not alone; we are part of a great body of believers, and what we do will affect many others, for good or evil.

(3) The unseen realm is more real than that which is seen: **"While we look not at the things which are seen, but at the things which are not seen; for the things which are seen**

are temporal, but the things which are not seen are eternal" (II Corinthians 4:18 NASB). Almost all of the weights and hindrances to our race come from the "seen" world, and their ability to hinder us only reveal that we are living more in the realm of the temporary than in that of the eternal.

(4)We should embrace the necessary discipline throughout our race. The author of Hebrews writes extensively in chapter 12 regarding God's disciplinary training of His children. If we are His, we will receive discipline because He disciplines everyone who belongs to Him. At the moment we receive it, chastisement is painful and may cause us sorrow. But we must keep in mind that the Lord's goal for this discipline is to provide us strength to run the race.

> Therefore, strengthen the hands that are weak and the knees that are feeble,
>
> and make straight paths for your feet, so that the limb which is lame may not be put out of joint, but rather healed (Hebrews 12:12,13 NASB).

Let Us Go to Jesus outside the Camp (Hebrews 13:13)

After the coming of the Holy Spirit on the day of Pentecost, the early believers continued going to Solomon's porch, a part of the temple, for their worship. As a result, many Jews were converted to Christ, angering the religious leaders of Jerusalem. Leaders of the "New Way" were persecuted, beaten and jailed. After the martyrdom of Stephen, the persecution reached a new fury which resulted in the scattering of believers from Jerusalem to all Judea.

Following Paul's encounter with Jesus on the road to Damascus, he returned to Jerusalem testifying for Christ. The church quickly sent him off in order to quiet the crowds. The peace that followed was actually a peace of compromise, but the church continued to grow—mixing Jewish rituals with Christian teachings. It seemed okay to be a Christian in Jerusalem as long as you didn't rock the religious boat.

When Paul returned from his third missionary trip, he was so anxious to worship with the church in Jerusalem, that he consented to observe the Nazarite vow of purifying himself. Upon his arrival he learned the Jerusalem church had fallen far from the times when they loved Jesus and followed the apostles' doctrine.

Thus when Jewish zealots tried to kill Paul, the church did not stand with him at all. They would not so much as bail him out of jail. I believe it was then that Paul went "without the camp" with Jesus. It had been proven once again that "new wine cannot be placed in old wine skins."

When churches become cold and unresponsive, the Lord raises up new apostles who will honor Him and provide new sheepfolds to meet the needs of the bleating sheep. At times, the Spirit of God will lead believers to remain with the old dried up wine skins as a testimony. However, others are either forced or led to go outside the present spiritual camp.

However, it is wisdom for everyone to examine his motives for remaining in the camp or for leaving it. Even David, a man after God's own heart, was willing to serve in the house of Saul until Saul drove him out. David did not leave the house of Saul in rebellion, and neither did he try to destroy Saul's house, or even speak ill of it, after so unjustly being driven out.

Even so, we must always keep in mind that the salvation of God did not come to save institutions; He came to save people. Institutions are to serve people, not the other way around. We should always be wary lest our devotion begins to be more for an institution than for the people. The Lord does not send His Spirit to make His people into better Baptists, better Methodists or even better Charismatics, but to make us all like His Son. He will obviously use any system as a channel for that purpose if allowed to do so, and those who are truly open to His Lordship and use are worthy of our honor and service, but not our worship.

The author of Hebrews saw the danger in the Hebrew believers remaining in a camp which was opposing the efficacy of the blood of Jesus and His work as their only High Priest. No one should leave a system because it is old nor join a new one because it is new, but there are times to leave the camp regardless of the reproach it might bring.

When we are motivated by the desire for men's approval it can destroy our confidence in the Lord and His promises. Speaking to those afraid of being put out of the synagogue for confessing Him, Jesus said: **"How can you believe, when you receive glory from one another, and you do not seek the glory that is from the one and only God?" (John 5:44 NASB).**

Just as He did with Stephen, the first Christian martyr, Jesus always reveals Himself in a special way to those who suffer and are persecuted for their faith in Him. For some to have a restoration of confidence, they must stop compromising with those who take the Word of God lightly—even if it means leaving the comfort of their religious camp. If we are to have true faith we must always esteem God's approval above man's.

Let Us Offer a Continual Sacrifice of Praise (Hebrews 13:15)

The author of Hebrews knew the pain in the souls of Christians who had gone "without the camp." They were even considered as dead and buried by close family members who were committed to the old religious traditions. No doubt these Jewish believers had difficulty singing or praising the Lord. But that is precisely when such praise is most meaningful to God, and when it will do the most for our own hearts.

Hosea had taught the Jews that when God put away their iniquities, they would make new sacrifices to the Lord—the offering of the fruit of their lips. Now these Jewish Christians were being admonished:

> **Through Him (Jesus) then, let us continually offer up a sacrifice of praise to God, that is, the fruit of lips that give thanks to His name. And do not neglect doing good and sharing; for with such sacrifices God is pleased (Hebrews 13:15,16 NASB).**

Praise is simply spoken confidence in our God. It is delightful when we feel within us a deep worship and praise to the Lord, but it is even more delightful to Him! Yet, there are times when the promises of God seem unfulfilled, prayers appear unanswered, difficulties abound. We are in danger of casting aside our confidence at that point. To praise at such a time will require sacrifice, which is why it is called "the sacrifice of praise." The Scriptures, from beginning to end, testify that sacrifice does get the attention of God. This is not to imply that it gets Him to notice us, as He is always fully aware of what happens even to each hair on our heads. But to get His attention is to get His response.

God is well pleased when we praise Him in every circumstance. We are to praise Him continually! That includes when we feel good and when we feel despair—*always*. We must understand that it can be even more meaningful when we do not feel like it! Most of us have been taught this as a doctrine. Now let us simply do what we know to do. If we cannot find words to praise God, then we can read a Psalm of praise, or get a hymn book and sing the words. This helps us to remove our attention from ourselves and onto Him who has the answers and the power to overcome every human circumstance. As we speak words of faith, our inner person will bear witness to our spoken faith and will generate confidence in our hearts.

Summary

We must be more than hearers or even readers of His Word. To receive the recompense of confidence, it is urgent to heed the admonitions of the Spirit. Three times the Hebrews were told: **"Today if you hear His voice, harden not your hearts ..."** **(Hebrews 3:7,15; 4:7).** If this chapter has been meaningful to you, please consider reading it again. Often we receive more the second time we read something than the first. Give earnest heed to the Spirit of the Lord. Paul exhorted the Corinthians: **"Having these promises, dearly beloved, let us cleanse**

ourselves from all filthiness of the flesh and spirit, perfecting holiness in the fear of God" (II Corinthians 7:1 NKJV).

So let us cultivate a healthy fear of the Lord. Let us be diligent, holding fast to our confession, and drawing near to God in bold assurance. Let us grow up in the body of the Lord, encouraging our brothers and sisters in Christ; running the race of faith. Let us go with Jesus outside the unbelieving religious camp. And last in this inventory, but among the uppermost in importance, come rain or sunshine, let's just keep praising the Lord, continuing to trust Him with confident and thankful hearts.

Chapter Nine

Confidence in the Sovereignty of God

The book of Habakkuk is the remarkable account of one man's journey from doubt to the worship of God. Habakkuk says those things that most of us have at least thought, especially at times when we did not understand what God was trying to achieve in our lives.

In Habakkuk's judgment, evil seemed to be victorious over good; iniquity and violence were everywhere. Even God's people were apathetic—often even rebellious. As is the case with many Christians, and even ministers, he was discouraged with the state of the world and the state of God's people.

As the book opens, the prophet expresses his discouragement with the circumstances around him:

O Lord, how long must I call for help before you will listen? I shout to you in vain; there is no

answer. "Help! Murder!" I cry, but no one comes to save. Must I forever see this sin and sadness all around me?

Wherever I look there is oppression and bribery and men who love to argue and to fight. The law is not enforced and there is no justice given in the courts, for the wicked far outnumber the righteous, and bribes and trickery prevail (Habakkuk 1:2-4 TLB).

Two crucial questions about God emerge from the first chapter: "Why doesn't God do something about evil? Why does God use wicked men in His dealings with His people?"

In response to Habakkuk's first question, the Lord responds that He will use the Chaldeans to deal with Israel. He describes the Chaldeans as: **"a bitter and hasty nation...they are terrible and dreadful...they all come for violence..."** **(Habakkuk 1:6-7,9 NKJV).**

God's answer to Habakkuk naturally induces a second question: **"Why do You look on those who deal treacherously, And hold Your tongue when the wicked devours a person more righteous than he?"** (verse 13, NKJV).

The Lord's response to Habakkuk's second question embraces a truth that is fundamental to the whole of the Christian faith: **"Behold the proud, His soul is not upright in him; But the just shall live by his faith"** (Habakkuk 2:4 NKJV).

The Jewish *Talmud* has stated: "Moses gave Israel 613 commandments." David reduced them to ten, Isaiah to two, but Habakkuk centers upon one—**"The just shall live by his faith" (Habakkuk 2:4)**

The Hebrew word for "shall live" is *chayah*- meaning: "to live; to stay alive; to be preserved; to flourish; to enjoy life; to live in happiness; to breathe; to be alive; to be animated; to recover health; to live continuously." That seems to cover just about everything.

Habakkuk 2:4 is quoted several times in the New Testament (Romans 1:17, Galatians 3:11, Hebrews 10:38). It is, in fact, the primary biblical truth that helped spark the Protestant Reformation. The verse literally reads: "The righteous person in (or by) his faithfulness (firmness, consistency, belief, faith, steadfastness) shall live!"

This verse can be a source of great strength to believers who are living through difficult times without the benefit of seeing the outcome ahead. In times of adversity and difficulty, we must trust that God is directing all things—even the ungodly—according to His purposes and divine plans. The Lord does at times use the ungodly to discipline His own people when they go astray, but Habakkuk 2:5-20 shows there are grave consequences for the greedy, the complacent, the violent, the shameless, and the idolaters.

Chapter 3 opens with the prophet returning to prayer before God. His conclusion in verses 17-19 brings him to a new-found confidence in spite of the circumstances and because of God Himself:

Even though the fig trees are all destroyed, and there is neither blossom left nor fruit, and though the olive crops all fail, and the fields lie barren; even if the flocks die in the fields and the cattle barns are empty, yet I will rejoice in the Lord; I will be happy in the God of my salvation. The Lord God is my Strength, and He will give me the speed of a deer and bring me safely over the mountains (TLB).

This is a remarkable statement of unconditional faith in God. Habakkuk's hope has been renewed. He is no longer controlled by his circumstances, but instead by faith in God's ability to provide. In the process, his anxiety has been lifted and he has traveled from complaining to confidence. He has experienced a transformation—typical of what the gospel itself brings into people's lives. Habakkuk has gone beyond the depression overpowering him into the joy of knowing God. He realizes that God is in charge even when it is not evident.

In verse 18, his new-found faith produces a rejoicing in the Lord: **"I will joy in the God of my salvation,"** he declares. The Hebrew word used for joy is *gil*. It means: "to joy, rejoice, be glad, be joyful." It contains the suggestion of "dancing for joy" or "leaping for joy." Concerning this word *gil,* the *Spirit Filled Life Bible* notes: "...the verb originally meant 'to spin around with intense motion.' This lays to rest the notion that the biblical concept of joy is only 'a quiet, inner sense of well-being.'"

Habakkuk provides strength and inspiration to all of us who have faced problems when nothing made sense and when troubles seemed overwhelming. Yet, God gives strength. He is sovereign. He is Lord. As we grasp this truth, we learn to take our eyes off the difficulties and look to God, who is **"...righteous in all his ways, and holy in all his works" (Psalm 145:17).**

Paul's Trouble & God's Sovereignty

The sixteenth chapter of the book of Acts records how the Holy Spirit led Paul and Silas along a missionary trip until they arrived in Philippi where Paul's greatest work in establishing a church would be proven. Later when Paul was jailed in Rome, he wrote a letter to the church at Philippi. A central verse of this book is Philippians 4:11 which states, **"I have learned, in whatsoever state I am, therewith to be content."**

We should note that contentment was something Paul had to learn. It did not come with his salvation experience. He certainly didn't have it when he got saved because the Lord's first words to him were: **"It is hard for thee to kick against the pricks" (Acts 9:5).** Paul had been a miserable man, fighting against the conviction of the Holy Spirit. Some people are in that misery because they are fighting the voice of God. Some even continue in this fight long after their salvation.

I am always faced with a number of questions when I read the opening verses of Philippians. How could Paul be so optimistic in the face of being without funds and in jail? How did he get to that place?

Now I want you to know, brothers, that what has happened to me has really served to advance the gospel.

As a result, it has become clear throughout the whole palace guard and to everyone else that I am in chains for Christ. Because of my chains, most of the brothers in the Lord have been encouraged to speak the word of God more courageously and fearlessly (Philippians 1:12-14 NIV).

Paul really looked at life through the eyes of Romans 8:28: **"And we know that in all things God works for the good of those who love him, who have been called according to his purpose" (Romans 8:28 NIV).** That is why he could say, "I am content and reigning in spite of the circumstances."

The Scripture does not say that all things are good. It doesn't even say that God brings all things into your life. It is obvious that the devil brings some things, and vile people bring a few things themselves. Yet, no matter what comes into your life and no matter who brings it, God says, "I will turn it around for good."

Paul understood this truth and that is why he could declare it—even from a Roman jail. He knew he loved the Lord and that God could break him out of jail at any time. It had happened once before at Philippi when an earthquake struck the prison.

If God is sovereign (and we believe He is), then nothing can happen without His knowledge of it, or without His ability to change it. This doctrine should not produce passivity in us to the point that we do not pray or assume our rightful place of dominion through Christ. We have spoken of our position in Christ and our ability in Him already. But it is not possible to remain content when it seems all hell has been turned loose on us unless we understand and believe that God is all powerful and is able at any time to intervene in our situations.

When Paul faced serious trouble in Jerusalem, the Roman commander of the city placed him in the army barracks to keep the Jews from killing him. While he was resting there, the Lord appeared to him and said: **"Take courage; for as you have solemnly witnessed to My cause at Jerusalem, so you must witness at Rome also" (Acts 23:11 NASB).**

I am sure those words comforted Paul in the days that followed. The Jews formed a conspiracy and bound themselves to an oath, saying they would neither eat nor drink until they had killed Paul. But they were not simply dealing and plotting against a man. They had to contend with the Sovereign Lord Himself, and He had declared that Paul would go to Rome. Nothing can stop the determination of God.

The Psalmist speaks strongly to us about the sovereignty of God:

> **Why are the nations in an uproar, and the peoples devising a vain thing?**

> **The kings of the earth take their stand, and the rulers take counsel together against the Lord and against His Anointed:**

> **He who sits in the heavens laughs, The Lord scoffs at them (Psalm 2:1,2,4 NASB).**

Who is like our God? There is no one who can stay His hand. There is absolutely nothing too hard for Him. When we consider God's greatness, we can sing with the Psalmist:

> **O Lord, our Lord, How majestic is Thy name in all the earth, Who hast displayed Thy splendor above the heavens!**
>
> **When I consider Thy heavens, the work of Thy fingers, the moon and the stars, which Thou hast ordained;**
>
> **What is man, that thou dost take thought of him? (Psalm 8:1,3,4 NASB).**

God Rules over All

Nebuchadnezzar was the most powerful Gentile king who ever lived, ruling over the immense and magnificent Babylonian Empire. Nebuchadnezzar continued in his boastings and pride even after dreaming his own downfall and later receiving Daniel's interpretation of the dream. For seven years, he was stark raving mad, roaming the fields and eating grass with the oxen, which worked to radically change his perspective:

> **But at the end of that period I, Nebuchadnezzar, raised my eyes toward heaven, and my reason returned to me, and I blessed the Most High and praised and honored Him who lives forever;**
>
> **for His dominion is an everlasting dominion, and His kingdom endures from generation to genera- tion...** *He does according to His will* **in the host of heaven and among the inhabitants of earth; and**

no one can ward off His hand or say to Him, "What hast Thou done?"

... All His works are true and His ways just, and He is able to humble those who walk in pride (Daniel 4:34-35,37b NASB).

This testimony comes from one who had not been a part of God's revelation to Abraham. He knew nothing of God's covenants. He was a pagan king of a pagan empire. Yet God in His sovereignty and His providence overruled the plans and destiny of the great Nebuchadnezzar, causing him to realize that with all his earthly authority and acclaim, he was a pygmy when compared with God Almighty. He bowed his knee and confessed Daniel's God as his Lord.

The sovereignty of God, when understood in balance, is absolutely the greatest peace-giving doctrine in all the Scriptures. In Him who created and rules over all, we can be confident. As Habakkuk wrote: **"The Lord is in his holy Temple; let all the earth be silent before Him" (Habakkuk 2:20 TLB).** This simply means: "When all is said and done, God will have the last word." He is the one and only God of all the universes, and every knee shall bow before Him. Because He is always just and always merciful and compassionate, we can be confident. He can and will bring His own into His loving, divine purposes. What a mighty God we serve!

Chapter Ten

Facing Death with Confidence

The central message of the early church was the resurrection of the Lord Jesus Christ. The disciples of the first century proclaimed: *"Jesus is not dead; He is alive...and because He lives, we are also alive forevermore."* Note Paul's words on this subject to the Corinthian church:

> ... **For your faith is squarely built upon this wonderful message; and it is this Good News that saves you if you still firmly believe it, unless of course you never really believed it in the first place.**

> **I passed on to you right from the first what had been told to me, that Christ died for our sins just as the Scriptures said he would, and that he was buried, and that three days afterwards he arose from the grave just as the prophets foretold...**

But tell me this! Since you believe what we preach, that Christ rose from the dead, why are some of you saying that dead people will never come back to life again? For if there is no resurrection of the dead, then Christ must still be dead...

But the fact is that Christ did actually rise from the dead, and has become the first of millions who will come back to life again some day.

Death came into the world because of what one man (Adam) did, and it is because of what this other man (Christ) has done that now there is the resurrection from the dead. Everyone dies because all of us are related to Adam, being members of his sinful race, and wherever there is sin, death results. But all who are related to Christ will rise again. Each, however, in his own turn: Christ rose first; then when Christ comes back, all his people will become alive again.

... If we will never live again after we die, then we might as well go and have ourselves a good time: let us eat, drink, and be merry. What's the difference? For tomorrow we die, and that ends everything!

The Scriptures tell us that the first man, Adam, was given a natural, human body but Christ is more than that, for he was life-giving Spirit.

First, then, we have these human bodies and later on God gives us spiritual, heavenly bodies.

I tell you this, my brothers: an earthly body made of flesh and blood cannot get into God's kingdom. These perishable bodies of ours are not the right kind to live forever. For our earthly bodies, the ones we have now that can die, must be transformed into heavenly bodies that cannot perish but will live forever (I Corinthians 15:1-4, 12,13, 20-23, 32b, 45,46, 50, 53 TLB).

The early followers of Jesus had their hope set upon Him driving out the pagan Gentile forces who ruled them and then setting up His kingdom in Israel. Thus, when He began speaking of His death, many rejected Him as the true Messiah. After all, if He was the promised Savior, how could He die? They knew of Elijah's rapture and how Enoch had been translated "that he should not see death." Surely after Jesus established His throne in Jerusalem, He would be caught up to heaven and rule from there.

After the Lord made a strong affirmation that He would **"go to Jerusalem, and suffer many things from the elders and chief priests and scribes, and be killed, and be raised up on the third day"** (Matthew 16:21, NASB), Peter challenged Him. In turn, Jesus rebuked Peter: **"Get behind Me, Satan! You are a stumbling block to Me; for you are not setting your mind on God's interests, but man's"** (verse 23).

The disciples did not understand Jesus' words and were perplexed at their meaning. He then set out to comfort and prepare them for His departure. His words in John 14:1,2 convey that effort of preparation:

> **Let not your heart be troubled; believe in God, believe also in Me. In My Father's house are many dwelling places; if it were not so, I would have told you; for I go to prepare a place for you (NASB).**

As a seminary student, I was told: "Don't be so heavenly minded, that you're no earthly good." The emphasis was well-timed as I was preparing for full-time ministry. The average evangelical was not the least bit interested in improving the society around him. Jesus was expected any day, and our priority was to get people ready for the rapture. There was no thought of being salt and light in this world, and we certainly would not have entertained the thought of going through the "great tribulation." But alas, it seems to me, the pendulum has now swung to the opposite extreme. The hope of heaven is seldom mentioned except in funeral sermons. Fewer today are excited about heaven than in those earlier days of preaching the imminent return of Jesus. Some even mock those who testify of heaven as "pie in the sky in the bye and bye" people.

It seems some present-day Christians want all their pie in the here and now. The emphasis is on having a beautiful home on earth and forgetting about our real home in heaven. In his classic book, *Mere Christianity*, C.S. Lewis wrote: "There is no need to be worried by facetious people who try to make the Christian hope of heaven ridiculous by saying they do not want to spend eternity playing harps."[1] Jesus never taught that we would spend eternity doing absolutely nothing. Nor did

He teach we would be floating around on clouds strumming harps or picking a ukulele. We have not yet been told precisely what we will be doing in eternity. However, the parables of Jesus strongly suggest we will be rewarded for our faithfulness to Him and will reign with Him over the whole creation.

In the book of Revelation, the apostle John describes Heaven as having celestial beauty beyond description. According to John, heaven will contain no more sea to separate nations, no more sun since Jesus will be the light, and no more tears since there will be nothing to bring pain. The apostle reveals a place with one language, peace everywhere, righteousness as white as snow, total understanding of God and His creation, and eternal health.

Paul was not even permitted to tell what he saw when he was caught up to heaven. Perhaps he knew his attempt to portray the sights would have been hopeless even with his great brilliance. However, there is no question that the greatest aspect of heaven will be the fellowship we will have with Jesus. According to John, the reality of seeing Jesus face-to-face should motivate us to personal purity:

> **See how great a love the Father has bestowed upon us, that we should be called children of God; and such we are. For this reason the world does not know us, because it did not know Him.**

> **Beloved, now we are children of God, and it has not appeared as yet what we shall be. We know that, when He appears, we shall be like Him, because we shall see Him just as He is.**

**And everyone who has this hope fixed on Him
purifies himself, just as He is pure (I John 3:1-3,
NASB).**

C.S.Lewis also wrote: "If you read history you will find
that Christians who did the most for the present world were
just those who thought most of the next...We shall never save
civilization as long as civilization is our main object. We must
learn to want something else even more."[2]

As pastor of a rural church some years ago, I preached the
funeral of an 11-year-old boy who had drowned. He had been
raised in church by devoted grandparents who taught him the
ways of the Lord. Accordingly, he had received Jesus as Lord
and was attentive in church services. His mother, who lived
elsewhere, was raised in a tradition where only the best saints
went to heaven when they died. Other nominal Christians had
to spend time in purgatory where they would be prepared for
heaven. She had not seen her son in some time and was
shocked by his death. I noticed that she was listening intently
to my message regarding believers who die, and particularly
the phrase **"to be absent from the body, and to be present
with the Lord" (II Corinthians 5:8).** Afterwards, she made
her way to me: "O, thank you for that wonderful message of
hope," she said, taking my hand. "I wish I could have that kind
of confidence. Roger is truly in the beautiful place you
described. In our religion, we don't hear the hope you
expressed."

Later I had the privilege of leading the woman to an
understanding of justification by faith which immediately
prepares a Christian to enter the presence of the Lord on earth

and in heaven. Such beliefs as those about a purgatory are the result of men really not believing that the blood of Jesus is enough to cleanse us from our sin and make us acceptable to God. Many believe that there must be some punishment that we must suffer to make us acceptable to the Father, but such thinking is an affront to the cross of our Savior who paid the full price. We will only be acceptable to the Lord because of the cross of Christ, not by our becoming purified by any other means. The cross is enough! We can put all of our trust in Jesus and the price that He paid to purchase us.

Heaven or Hell

"It is appointed unto men once to die, but after this the judgment" (Hebrews 9:27). We are all terminal. The only exceptions to this are believers who are alive at the coming of Jesus who will be changed instantly from a mortal body to an immortal one. Since each one of us must die and then face the Lord, it is ever so important that our confidence and hope of life after death be based on Scriptural truth and on nothing else. According to Jesus, everyone will come forth from the grave and spend eternity in either heaven or hell (see John 5:28,29). When Nicodemus, who was a Pharisee, came to Jesus for an explanation of how His miracles were performed, Jesus stated in no uncertain terms:

> **... truly, truly, I say unto you, unless one is born again, he cannot see the kingdom of God.**

> **Do not marvel that I said to you, "You must be born again."**

For God so loved the world that He gave His only begotten Son, that whoever believes in Him should not perish, but have eternal life.

He who believes in the Son has eternal life; but he who does not obey the Son shall not see life, but the wrath of God abides on him (John 3:3,7,16,36 NASB).

There is only one way to be saved and to have eternal life—to believe in Jesus and to acknowledge the price that He paid for our sins. The apostle Peter boldly stood before the Sanhedrin in Jerusalem and declared: **"And there is salvation in no one else; for there is no other name under heaven that has been given among men, by which we must be saved"** (Acts 4:12 NASB).

Therefore we must not only preach about eternity in Heaven, we must warn the world of the realities of Hell. Martin Luther said, "Before a man can appreciate Heaven, he needs to dangle over Hell awhile." John Wesley said, "Anyone who desires to be admitted into these societies (Methodist societies which later became The Methodist Church) should first desire to flee the wrath to come and be saved from all his sins." That kind of preaching may seem too old fashioned for the present day world, but it may help to know that John Wesley was so sure of his message, he rode over 200,000 miles on horseback preaching the whole counsel of God. He died at eighty plus years still preaching and singing praises to the Lord.

Jesus often mentioned the existence and torments of Hell in His teachings; then He took our sins upon Himself and suffered the pains and eternal retribution of Hell for us on the cross. The real good news is that Jesus saves anyone who receives Him as Lord from the penalty of sin. He delivers those who believe in Him from the wrath to come and consequently takes away their fear of death.

The Nature of Death

In His response to the Sadducees who did not believe in life after death, Jesus said:

> **But regarding the resurrection of the dead, have you not read that which was spoken to you by God, saying, "I am the God of Abraham, and the God of Isaac, and the God of Jacob." He is not the God of the dead but of the living (Matthew 22:31,32 NASB).**

The writer of Hebrews likewise affirmed:

> **Since then the children share in flesh and blood, He Himself likewise also partook of the same, that through death He might render powerless him who had the power of death, that is, the devil;**
>
> **and might deliver those who through fear of death were subject to slavery all their lives (Hebrews 2:14,15 NASB).**

The nature of God is life. The nature of Satan is death. When man fell to Satan's deception, he came under the power of death and the fear of death. Jesus became a man that He might defeat the devil and destroy the power of death. Since death was passed to all humanity by Adam, the only way for

Jesus to save us from death was to take on the nature of man and overcome Satan in the flesh. Jesus entered into every condition of fallen humanity—yet He never sinned. So, through death, Jesus took on the penalty of sin, which is death. At Calvary, Jesus broke the power of the devil, and now we can have complete deliverance from the fear of death. **"Death is swallowed up in victory" (I Corinthians 15:54 NASB).**

Ready to Depart

When Nero issued the death penalty over Paul's life, the apostle faced death with confidence:

> **For I am already being poured out as a drink offering, and the time of my departure has come.**
>
> **I have fought the good fight, I have finished the course, I have kept the faith;**
>
> **in the future there is laid up for me the crown of righteousness, which the Lord, the righteous Judge, will award to me on that day; and not only to me, but also to all who have loved His appearing (II Timothy 4:6-8 NASB).**

The word "departure" which Paul used to describe his impending death is *analusis*, meaning "a dissolving into separate parts" or "an unloosing." It is also a nautical term which means "loosing from moorings," or it can be used as a military term denoting "breaking up camp." So, Paul considered his death as leaving for another port, or another camp. Peter also spoke freely and with confidence of his departure:

Knowing that the laying aside of my earthly dwelling is imminent, as also our Lord Jesus Christ has made clear to me. And I will also be diligent that at any time after my departure you may be able to call these things to mind (II Peter 1:14,15 NASB).

Peter used a different word *exodon* when he learned of his approaching death for Christ. The word is also used to speak of the Lord's death in Luke 9:31. It means to go out from one place to another. Thus, we are to think of those who have died in faith as being in another room or another city. As a result, we are not to sorrow as those who have no hope. Whether in natural death, martyrdom—or even as a criminal on death row—each believer can be confident of immediate life with Jesus Christ and fellowship with every family member who has gone before.

Apostle of Death Row

In 1981 Larry Heath was convicted in a Georgia court of hiring hit-men to kill his wife who was then nine months pregnant. He was sentenced to life in prison. Afterwards, he was extradited to Alabama where he was convicted of hiring the kidnapper from that state and was sentenced to death. Ten years of attempting to prove double jeopardy in the case ultimately failed, and Larry was executed at Holman Prison in Atmore, Alabama on March 20, 1992.

After his conversion in 1982, Larry became a witness to inmates, guards, and officers at the prison. Over the next ten years, he graduated from six major correspondence Bible Schools, including Moody, Rhema, and Berean. Some tried to portray him as a con man attempting to influence the courts with "jail house religion" in order to escape the electric chair.

Larry's answer was simple: "I live with cons 24 hours a day, and you can't con a con." Other death row inmates called him the "Apostle of Death Row" because of the love, peace, and joy visible in his life. They knew he was not a counterfeit professor of Christ.

A few weeks before the final appeal for life without parole was denied by the U.S. Supreme Court, the Prison's Chaplain and two other pastors made a request to Liberty Fellowship for Larry's ordination as a minister of the gospel. According to Liberty pastors who ministered in the prison and knew Larry, he had been a tremendous witness for the Lord and had won many inmates to Christ. He had even had a great influence on guards and others who worked on death row.

We unanimously agreed to ordain Larry, and as Founder and Advising Pastor of Liberty Fellowship, I conducted the ordination service in the death row section at the prison on February 27, 1992. Never in 41 years of preaching had I ever ministered on a prison death row. The atmosphere in the prison halls was gloomy, and a few men in nearby cells were noisy. Yet, the twenty inmates who attended the service were cheerful and attentive. Their worship matched any church service on the outside. I preached the ordination service after four other ministers who knew Larry spoke. Then, we laid hands on Larry, recognizing him as a true minister of the gospel. For the first time, I heard Larry speak about the Lord, offering thanks for his salvation and the opportunity to work for Him in prison.

According to Buford Lipscomb, a Liberty pastor who had befriended Larry, the entire prison was "abuzz" for days about this ordination service. That was the last time I saw Larry;

exactly one month from that day, he was executed. Buford Lipscomb, Liberty Fellowship District Overseer for South Alabama, provided the story of Larry's final day on earth:

> The chaplain called me during the night, telling me that Larry had been moved from his cell to the holding cell next to the death chamber. When I arrived on Thursday morning, Larry met me at the door of his holding cell... For the benefit of the other inmates around him, he didn't want any good-byes said. It had been a tough night. Larry wanted to talk about memorial services. He reminded me if some of what he wanted to discuss was too much, I should say so. We continued and completed the plans for the local memorial service and a service to be held for the family in Birmingham.
>
> I struggled deeply about whether I should make arrangements to view the execution or not. I received a wide range of counsel, but I told Larry, "I feel I should go all the way with you. We've gone too far together for me to back off now."
>
> Arrangements were made with prison officials for a communion service to be held at 7:30 that night. The only ones present for the service were Larry's family, his two attorneys, the chaplain, assistant chaplain, Jim Britnell (a Liberty Fellowship minister), and myself. Jim was in charge of the service. Larry had told him he did not want to say anything, but changed his mind during the worship and shared from his heart about the power of the cross. With tears streaming down his face, he told us these ten years had been the happiest of his life. He confirmed his love for all.
>
> One of Larry's attorneys stood and confessed Christ as his Savior for the first time during the communion. His

final words to Larry were, "You can face what you must tonight knowing your life has been used to bring me to the Lord."

As we returned to the cell, the chaplain was on one side of Larry and I was on the other. Two pairs of officers marched ahead of us and three pairs behind. All that could be heard was the echo of our footsteps, with guards and inmates frozen in position as we walked by. Before Larry was placed in the cell, he did a remarkable thing. He went to each officer, individually shook his hand or hugged his neck and told him how much he appreciated his care all through the years.

Larry had made arrangements with the warden for a stereo to play his favorite songs after he was placed in his cell. The tape, *His Last Days* about the life of Jesus, concludes with the song "Rise Again." The music filled the entire death row wing of the prison captivating inmates and guards alike. An awesome presence of God hovered so near.

We fellowshipped and talked over and over about how we felt the peace of God among us. At 11 p.m. they came to shave Larry's head and left leg. At one point, Larry remarked: "I knew I would have a peace, but I never dreamed it would be like this." He held his hands out for us to see. "Look! My hands are not even shaking. There is no fear in me." When the guard announced it was time, Larry stood and whispered in my ear: "We'll finish our conversation in heaven."

While the guards prepared Larry for execution, the blinds in the chamber were lowered and I was seated with the other witnesses. When the blinds were raised, Larry was smiling at us. A lengthy death warrant was read by the warden, and then he asked Larry if he had any final words. Larry responded: "As a matter of fact, I do." He spoke for fifteen minutes addressing the warden, the head of corrections for the State of Alabama, and others with words of kindness. He then addressed the press: "I know you all have been highly skeptical and have not believed my testimony. I want you to know I bear no hard feelings." He commented to the victim's family that maybe now they would be able to forgive him. His voice never cracked as he ended his statements and prayed for everyone there.[3]

Those were Larry Heath's final words on earth. He entered into heaven with full confidence in his Lord. His reason for execution was not the same as Paul's or Peter's, (though Paul was a murderer of Christians before his conversion), but the confidence was the same. Jesus had taken away the fear of death.

Come Forth!

When Jesus was in Judea, He spent much of His time with Lazarus and his two sisters, Mary and Martha, at their home in Bethany. The sisters considered Him their special friend, and so it was quite natural when Lazarus became sick, they sent for Jesus, thinking He would come quickly.

But the Lord deliberately waited until He knew Lazarus had died and had been buried for four days. Then He took His disciples there to witness the raising of Lazarus from the dead. It is from the Lord's conversation with the two sisters (see John 11) that we learn much about life after death and the immediate state of those who have died in faith.

Not only were the two sisters grieving over their brother's death, but they harbored some resentment that Jesus did not come immediately when He received word about Lazarus. When Martha heard that Jesus was in the village, she hurried out to meet Him:

> **Martha therefore said to Jesus, "Lord, if You had been here, my brother would not have died."**
>
> **Jesus said to her, "Your brother shall rise again."**
>
> **Martha said to Him, " I know that he will rise again in the resurrection on that last day" (John 11:21,23,24 NASB).**

It was then that Jesus spoke those cherished words engraved in the hearts of believers everywhere: **"I am the resurrection and the life; he who believes in Me shall live even if he dies, and everyone who lives and believes in Me shall never die. Do you believe this?" (verses 25,26 NASB).**

A good question indeed! Do you believe this? Do you *really* believe this? For if you believe this, why be afraid of death or grieve over the death of those you love? If you *really* believe this, you can face death as though you were moving to another, better room. This physical body is a tabernacle which clothes you as long as you live on earth. Our inner being, our spirit, will someday move out of this house of clay, as Paul stated in II Corinthians 5:4-8:

> **For indeed while we are in this tent, we groan, being burdened, because we do not want to be**

unclothed, but to be clothed, in order that what is mortal may be swallowed up by life.

Now He who prepared us for this very purpose is God, who gave to us the Spirit as a pledge.

Therefore, being always of good courage, and knowing that while we are at home in the body we are absent from the Lord—

for we walk by faith, not by sight—

we are of good courage, I say, and prefer rather to be absent from the body and to be at home with the Lord (NASB).

We can be of "good courage" in the face of death. We can have confidence. When Jesus called for Mary, she came and fell weeping at His feet. Jesus said nothing to her. Perhaps He was too stirred with compassion to speak. John writes: **"... He was deeply moved in spirit, and was troubled and said, 'Where have you laid him?' They said to Him, 'Lord, come and see.' Jesus wept"** (John 11:33-35 NASB).

After a time of prayer, He told the disciples to remove the stone over the grave. Standing before the cave, He spoke with a loud voice: **"Lazarus, come forth"** (verse 43). And he did! Someone has said that if Jesus had not spoken the name "Lazarus," every believer who had ever died would have come forth from his grave. One day He will shout those same words "Come forth" and the "dead (bodies) in Christ shall rise." Death has lost its sting. The grave has lost its victory. Christ is alive forevermore and has the keys of Hell and death. We are more than conquerors even over man's last enemy, and our confidence without reservation is that those in Christ shall never, never die.

> **For I am convinced that neither death, nor life, nor angels, nor principalities, nor things present, nor things to come, nor powers,**
>
> **nor height, nor depth, nor any other created thing, shall be able to separate us from the love of God, which is in Christ Jesus our Lord (Romans 8:38,39 NASB).**

This confidence is the secret to overwhelming victory in this life and in the life to come.

Chapter Eleven

Keep Your Confidence

What should we do when our prayers are not being answered as quickly as we desire? No matter what the need is—an illness, a financial problem or an unsaved friend—the answer is the same; we must keep our confidence in the Lord. Hebrews 3:14 declares: **"For we are made partakers of Christ, if we hold the beginning of our confidence steadfast unto the end" (NASB).**

The writer of Hebrews further admonishes us to hold on to our confidence, because we need patience to do His will so that we can receive what has been promised:

Cast not away therefore your confidence, which hath great recompense of reward. For ye have need of patience, that, after ye have done the will of God, ye might receive the promise (Hebrews 10:35,36).

The patience mentioned in this scripture is not passive, although it is often interpreted that way. Patience involves steadfastness and endurance. It is an action word. We have seen that God alone is the source of real and lasting confidence.

167

Let us now examine the necessary steps to retaining the God-kind of confidence.

(1) **We must deal with disappointments quickly.** Many people do not grasp this truth and wind up becoming mortally wounded because they have allowed hurt to build up in their lives.

There are many people, even in the church, who are angry at God for some disappointment or discouragement which has happened in their lives. They think since God is Almighty and could have prevented the tragedy, somehow He is at fault and is to be blamed. When this kind of attitude prevails in the church, the result is discouragement, bitterness and defeat in the lives of God's people.

Whatever the reason for our disappointment with the Lord, the best approach is for us to tell Him about it. Of course He knows anyway, but it will help us. We can go to Him with our disappointment. When we seek Him we will find Him, and we will usually find the answers to our questions. We must never run from God, but to Him.

The same is true of the church. The church is composed of people, and even the best of people will disappoint us at times, even if it is unintentional. If we would learn to deal with these disappointments quickly, they would seldom escalate into serious divisions. Also, we can be sure that as often as we have been disappointed, we have very likely disappointed others. This is true even if we cannot remember doing it, which is one reason why we have disappointed others—we forget our commitments!

(2) **We must resist condemnation.** Condemnation is a primary enemy of our confidence. Proverbs 28:1 states: **"...the righteous are bold as a lion" (NASB).** The lion is probably the most confident animal in the jungle, and God's Word says we should emulate the lion with our confidence. This is hard to do when we are carrying a heavy load of guilt. If we are carrying such guilt it is simply because we have not taken it to the cross.

If we are in Christ we should be as confident in our relationship to God on our bad days as we are on our good days. This is not because our behavior is meaningless, but because *Jesus paid the price for our sin.* Our relationship to God is not based on how good we are, but on the perfect sacrifice that Jesus made for us.

Peter and Judas both failed the Lord on the night of His passion. Peter turned to the Lord, was restored, and the humility of his failure enabled him to be even more greatly used by the Lord. His humility was not demonstrated by continued remorse, but by an increased dependency on the Lord.

Judas could have likewise been forgiven for his failure. It is obvious that he felt great remorse for his sin, but he did not turn to Jesus—he tried to pay the price for his own sin. For this he was called "incorrigible," which means that he was beyond help. What made him incorrigible was not the sin, but his determination to pay the price for it himself, which no man can do. Like Judas, many people, even "believers," refuse to go to Jesus with their sins, but feel that they must pay the price for them with extended guilt.

The power of God resides in the cross, and that is the only place where we will find the grace to overcome the sin. When we try to pay the price for our own sins by carrying the guilt ourselves, it actually weakens us to the sin so that we will continue to fall. Those who try to carry their own guilt will inevitably fall to legalism, or they will give up and fall to license.

(3) **We must not dwell on defeat or distress.** In spite of all the problems confronting this world, we must learn not to dwell upon them but to concentrate on how God can work His purpose in them, or in spite of them.

There are many problems in the world today that cause us great turmoil—people starving all over the world, the population explosion, wars in many lands, crime in our streets. Could it be that God has a plan in the face of all these insufferable situations? It is often the very problems we face that bring people back to God. Our God rules over the entire universe, and He will prevail. It is only when we become overly concerned with the temporary that we begin to fall to petty defeats. In Christ, even our defeats are used for our good, and we must always keep our attention on His (and our) ultimate victory.

(4) **We must not trust our feelings.** We must learn to trust the Word of God above our feelings. Our feelings can depend on countless factors including what we ate for supper, how we slept last night, the good or bad news we just received. It is wonderful to feel good, but regardless of how we feel, we must esteem the Word of God as the ultimate reality.

We are called to walk by faith, not by sight. The Lord promises that He will never leave us or forsake us, but that does not mean that we will be able to "feel" His presence all of the time. He does not dwell in our feelings; He dwells in our hearts, and they are not the same. King David expressed it in Psalm 139:7-10:

> **Whither shall I go from thy spirit? or whither shall I flee from thy presence?**
>
> **If I ascend up into heaven, thou art there: if I make my bed in hell, behold, thou art there.**
>
> **If I take the wings of the morning, and dwell in the uttermost parts of the sea;**
>
> **Even there shall thy hand lead me, and thy right hand shall hold me.**

We must learn to take God at His Word. If we seek God, He promises to be found by us, but He does not promise to always be "felt" by us. If we draw nigh to Him, He will draw nigh to us.

(5) <u>**We must allow our minds to be renewed.**</u> Having our minds renewed is vital if we are to walk in this world with true biblical confidence instead of just a cheap substitute. When we receive Jesus Christ as Lord, and are born again by the Spirit, that instant we become a child of God—a new creature in Christ. When we are born again we instantly begin to see the world from an entirely different perspective. However, we then often fall right back into our previous perspective because of "the tyranny of the familiar." It is simply very difficult to break old habits. That is why the renewing of our minds is a process that we work out day by day. But it is important that we do continue in this process and not just succumb to our old ways of thinking.

The apostle Paul wrote to the Romans: **"And do not be conformed to this world, but be transformed by the renewing of your mind..." (Romans 12:2 NASB)**. He told the Ephesians: **"... be renewed in the spirit of your mind" (Ephesians 4:23 NASB)**. The greatest battlefield for the Christian is in the mind! We are never any better than what we think.

> **For the weapons of our warfare are not carnal, but mighty through God to the pulling down of strongholds;**
>
> **casting down imaginations (reasonings), and every high thing that exalteth itself against the knowledge of God, and bringing into captivity every thought to the obedience of Christ (II Corinthians 10:4,5).**

These two verses tell us the following:

(1) Our battle with Satan is primarily in the mind.
(2) We can win only if we use God's divine means in this warfare.
(3) There are strongholds in our minds which are in conflict with the knowledge of God.
(4) Any thought contrary to the Scriptures must be considered an enemy and resisted by casting it down.
(5) We must make every thought bow to the Lordship of Jesus Christ.

Whether we live in victory or defeat as Christians will depend upon how effectively we battle against the strongholds built in our minds by the ways of this world in which we live. Some of the more common strongholds which must be dealt with are selfish thoughts (Matthew 16:23), prejudiced thoughts (Acts 10:34), lustful thoughts (Titus 1:15), anxious thoughts (Matthew 6:25) childish thoughts (I Corinthians 13:11), and accusing thoughts.

After we have cast down the strongholds in our minds, we must then make a deliberate effort to renew our minds. **"Gird your minds for action" (I Peter 1:13 NASB).** There will be defeat in our greatest spiritual battle until we determine that we will have a transformed thought life. To be passive is to be defeated. To do this is to **"fight the good fight of faith" (I Timothy 6:12 NASB).** We must set our minds **"on the things above, not on the things that are on the earth" (Colossians 3:2 NASB).** The apostle exhorted the church at Philippi:

> **Finally, brethren, whatever is true, whatever is honorable, whatever is right, whatever is pure, whatever is lovely, whatever is of good repute, if there is any excellence and if anything worthy of praise, let your mind dwell on these things (Philippians 4:8 NASB).**

(6) **We must cultivate a desire for God Himself.** The greatest confidence that we can have in this life will come from our intimacy with God. If we know that we are known by God, what men may think of us will not make any difference to us. If we know that we are children of the King of Kings, we will not be impressed, or intimated by even the world's most powerful people.

The greatest promise in the Bible must certainly be that if we seek God we will find Him, and if we draw near to Him, He will draw near to us. He declared through Jeremiah:

For I know the thoughts that I think toward you, saith the Lord, thoughts of peace, and not of evil, to give you an expected end.

Then shall ye call upon me, and ye shall go and pray unto me, and I will hearken unto you.

And ye shall seek me, and find me, when ye shall search for me with all your heart (Jeremiah 29:10-13).

We are promised that we will find Him when we seek Him with all of our hearts. To what better pursuit could we ever give ourselves? We are all as close to God as we want to be. The Source of our confidence, and everything else that we will ever truly need, is available to each one of us. Man was created to have fellowship with God who is Spirit, and there will be a deep void in all of our lives until we are intimate with Him again. We all try to fill that void many other ways, but none will ever satisfy except the Lord Jesus Himself.

And this is the confidence that we have in him, that, if we ask any thing according to his will, he heareth us: And if we know that he hear us, whatsoever we ask, we know that we have the petitions that we desired of him (I John 5:14,15).